# MINDS OVER MATTER

By JEFFREY ROTHFEDER

Computer Book Division/Simon & Schuster, Inc.
New York

Published by the Computer Book Division
Simon & Schuster, Inc.
Simon & Schuster Building
Rockefeller Center
1230 Avenue of the Americas
New York, New York 10020
SIMON AND SCHUSTER and colophon are registered trademarks
of Simon & Schuster, Inc.
Designed by Bernard Stone
Manufactured in the United States of America

10 9 8 7 6 5 4 3 2 1

Library of Congress Cataloging in Publication Data
Rothfeder, Jeffrey.
Minds over matter.

Bibliography: p.
1. Artificial intelligence. 2. Computers.
I. Title.
Q335.R69 1985 001.53'5 85-3625
ISBN 0-671-53206-5

Grateful acknowledgement is made to the following for permission to reprint previously published material:

Addison-Wesley Publishing Company, Inc.: Excerpts reprinted from *The Fifth Generation,* by Edward Feigenbaum and Pamela McCorduck. Copyright © 1983. Reprinted by permission of the publisher.

The Massachusetts Institute of Technology: Excerpts reprinted from AI Memo 660 (1982), *How to Play Twenty Questions with Nature and Win,* by Whitman Richards. Reprinted by permission of the author.

North Holland Publishing Company: Excerpts reprinted from *Computer Compacts,* Volume 1:6 (1984). Reprinted by permission of the publisher.

# ACKNOWLEDGMENTS

This book would have been impossible to write without the estimable cooperation of so many people in the artificial-intelligence community who freely shared the most intimate details of their lives' work. In this regard, I owe special gratitude to Stephen Andriole, Ernest Kent, Joseph Weizenbaum, Edward Feigenbaum, Jaime Carbonell, Whitman Richards, Robert Bolles, Ronald Cain and Roger Schank. Additionally, thanks are due to the excellent public relations people and researchers—in the latter group, particularly Mitch Marcus and Mark Lavin—at Bell Labs and IBM. It was pleasing to see, in this age of cynicism about the motives of corporate giants, that two of the largest companies in the world are keeping few basic research secrets from the public.

My researcher for this book, Eva Waskell, deserves special mention and thanks. She is one of the best researchers in the country in the neurosciences, advanced computers and artificial intelligence. Ms. Waskell has the uncanny ability to take the most complex scientific theories, home in on their significant aspects and describe their importance to laypeople and scientists alike. She is about to embark on a book-writing career of her own; it will no doubt be an excellent one.

Finally—and most importantly—I'd like to acknowledge the participation of Dorie MacDonald in the preparation of this book. Her support, patience, editing, questioning, proofreading and encouragement kept this project going, especially during some of its most crucial periods.

# CONTENTS

**Introduction:** An Electronic Synthesis ..... **9**

**Chapter 1:** Dartmouth 1956 .............. **15**

**Chapter 2:** Turing's Failed Legacy ......... **26**

**Chapter 3:** The Second Wave .............. **39**

**Chapter 4:** On Mining Heuristics and Knowledge ......................... **69**

**Chapter 5:** Language, Learning and Scripts ........................... **114**

**Chapter 6:** Twenty Questions—Organizing a Disorganized Universe .. **150**

**Chapter 7:** Those Who Pay the Freight ... **182**

**Chapter 8:** The Human Variable ......... **219**

**Further Reading** ...................... **227**

# Introduction

# AN ELECTRONIC SYNTHESIS

At first glance, the press conference did not appear to be noteworthy. In mid–1984, to a largely uninterested group, the head of a General Motors automobile manufacturing branch described in detail why GM had bought a minority interest in a small computer-and-software firm in California. GM intended, he explained, to use the computer company's expertise and equipment to speed the arrival of the car of the future. Hyperbole is expected at such briefings. Cars of the future are announced regularly—although they either never appear or when they do, they are not much different from the car of yesterday. But there was something more, much more, to the GM official's statements that went generally unnoticed.

For one thing, GM's futuristic automobile would be as smart as a crack automobile mechanic. It would understand its own engine and peripheral parts in the same way that people know how their bodies work. The computer embedded in the auto would have the ability to reach diagnostic conclusions based on subtle changes in the performance of components. It would know, for instance, when cylinders were failing, perhaps months before they would actually be rendered unusable.

More importantly, beneath the rhetoric of GM's announcement lies buried the implication that consumers will soon be commonly using a revolutionary computer technology: artificial intelligence.

The new science of artificial intelligence seeks to create computers that think and react to information and are ultimately able to reach wholly unique and accurate conclusions for any given situation. It is an endeavor to make computers that are unlike any others we have known up to now; computers that would, in every sense, possess intelligence.

Though creating artificial intelligence may seem at first blush to be the outlandish fantasy of god-playing researchers, teaching cognitive skills to computers in the laboratory is turning out to be a practical process of machine education. In fact, the achievements of artificial-intelligence research to date are even more significant than any ballyhoo about the car of the future would suggest. The smart automobile is nothing but a mere detail on the discipline's lofty and partially completed agenda. There are already primitive computers that possess medical diagnostic skills; others that understand language and learn from conversations with people or by reading texts; and robots with sight that are able to distinguish objects, even those hidden in complicated scenery or lying among similar objects.

As a research aim, creating intelligent machines is, obviously, a goal of no small measure. Indeed, if fully accomplished, it would permanently change society and affect scientific evolution. But there is an equally powerful byproduct resulting from artificial-intelligence research: it is offering unique and detailed views of the way the human mind works.

Research on the human mind is generally a slow process, requiring severe diligence in methods used and equally burdensome testing time frames. Neuroscientists and behavioral psychologists constantly battle with an imposing research dilemma: Any conclusions or hypotheses they reach are excruciatingly difficult to test. The hard-won theories these researchers arrive at to describe the brain's intricate networking and its ability to process information and knowledge take years to test out and prove on human subjects.

Ironically, the study of artificial intelligence is finally presenting a way out of this hammerlock. Researchers have discovered that as they examine the foundations of people's intelligence and transfer their insights onto computers, they are at the same time creating some of the best models of the mind yet devised. In effect, the validity of emerging theories of mind can be analyzed far more quickly than ever by studying how well these theories perform on computers. Already in artificial intelligence's short history, its contribution to mind research has been considerable.

Artificial intelligence is a bold enterprise. As a discipline, it is taking on the centuries-long religious, philosophical and technological debates over whether machines are equal to man. Researchers in the discipline are optimistic that they are about to put this argument to rest. Their conclusion is that, indeed, the machine will measure up to man.

This is not to say that the chronology of artificial intelligence has been without its share of stammers. And despite its series of recent successes, much more is left to be done. Hundreds of millions of dollars have already been poured into the field by the federal government and interested high-technology corporations. Hundreds of millions more will be spent before the primitively intelligent computers of today are turned into mature machines that, in fully human ways, learn, reason, make judgments, understand language and see.

Since monetary backing is not difficult to obtain, the discipline can afford the services of some of the most impressive computer technologists in the nation. Among them:

*Roger Schank, the head of the computer science department at Yale University, who, by tutoring computers in the wellsprings of language, is teaching them the rubrics of learning and formulating original knowledge.*

*Edward Feigenbaum, a professor at Stanford University, who has studied extensively how physicians, atomic-bonding researchers and chemists reach conclusions and is successfully transferring this knowledge into computer memories.*

*Ronald Cain and Robert Bolles, both of the Stanford Research Institute think tank, who are dissecting vision, perhaps the most difficult of human mental skills, and with the power of video are enabling computers to see.*

*Ernest Kent, formerly of the University of Illinois and now hacking for the Defense Department, who is combining computer vision with human learning and memory techniques to create a machine that not only identifies the objects it sees but teaches itself the properties of new shapes it comes across.*

*Jaime Carbonell, a computer scientist at Carnegie-Mellon University, who holds that people use analogies to teach themselves original concepts throughout their lives. Carbonell is writing programs that allow a computer to access analogies from its memory, based on those humans use, so that it can learn the meaning of new ideas.*

Today, artificial-intelligence researchers are openly optimistic. Although the discipline has been labored over since the end of the 1940s (when it was known as *cybernetics*) and was officially kicked off in 1956, this is the first time that its optimistic rhetoric bears signs of truth. Some of the leading names in computer history—including Warren McCulloch, Walter Pitts, Nobel Prize-winner Herbert Simon, Allen Newell, and the "grandfather" of computing, Alan Turing—have peppered the history of artificial intelligence, promising constantly that they had found the key to achieve machine intelligence. They were each time sadly mistaken in their projections and off-base in the central assumptions of their theories. More often than not, they attempted to force-feed utterly baseless theories of how the mind works into computer programs. These ill-conceived theories were usually derived from the erroneous idea that the mind is built along the same lines as the mathematically rigorous, early-generation computing machines. The results, in hindsight, were predictably less than satisfactory.

Fortunately, artificial-intelligence researchers today have rejected the misguided direction followed by their forebears in the discipline. The present crop of researchers correctly feel that if the discipline had continued down the path on which it had originally embarked, it would have sputtered to a halt as just another interesting fantasy in our pipedreams about cloning man's mind.

But as the GM announcement indicated, artificial intelligence is reaching maturity. As this look at artificial intelligence—its history, its failures and successes, its theories of mind and its leading practitioners—reveals, we are now witnessing a remarkable technological synthesis.

# Chapter 1

# DARTMOUTH 1956

Though conceived about a decade earlier, artificial intelligence was finally born in 1956 at a summer-long conference held at Dartmouth University. For nearly two months, two dozen men congregated in the sun-parched hills of Hanover, New Hampshire, staking out the legitimate boundaries for their new scientific discipline.

Dubbed the Dartmouth Summer Research Project on Artificial Intelligence, it was mostly a time of rubbing shoulders for these artificial-intelligence researchers who had labored up to then in anonymity. The small group of conferees had invested long hours since the early 1950s at academic centers like Harvard and Carnegie-Tech, corporations like IBM and AT&T and think tanks like the Rand Corporation, pursuing an esoteric, mostly unknown science. They came to New Hampshire hoping to share knowledge with each other and define the issues that would shape the discipline.

In many ways Dartmouth was a funding drive for artificial intelligence. Full-scale backing from government agencies, private research foundations and academic laboratories is never given for long periods to the less-than-useful sciences. Funding depends, instead, on a recognized track record of progress toward a well-defined and meaningful goal. Until 1956, artificial intelligence had been financed on a shoestring. The Dartmouth conference, it was hoped, would catch the eye of the major funding agencies who, in turn, would pay the first installment on the future of artificial intelligence.

This, in fact, is precisely what happened. And in hindsight it represents the only tangible result of the Dartmouth conference. Primarily because of that two-month meeting, artificial intelligence was lifted out of the obscurity of university and corporate research laboratories and given at least a modicum of public prominence and a significant amount of financial support. Little, however, if anything in the way of scientific import took place at Dartmouth.

Had this analysis of the New Hampshire conclave been spoken in 1956, it would have been distinctly a minority opinion, disparaged as heresy. Most of the artificial-intelligence researchers left the conference enthused and full of bravado. Some of them felt they were on the verge of riding the same heady course of public acclaim as their contemporaries, the mappers of DNA.

Consider a statement made soon after the convention: "It is not my aim to surprise or shock you, but the simplest way I can summarize it is to say that there are now in the world machines that think, that learn, and that create. Moreover, their ability to do these things is going to increase rapidly until—in a visible future—the range of problems they can handle will be coextensive with the range to which the human mind has applied them." Herbert Simon, at that time working for Carnegie-Tech and Rand and since then the winner of a Nobel Prize in economics, wrote these words just a few months after the Dartmouth conference.

Though he was wrong—there were no machines (and there still are none) that in full dimensions think, learn and create—Simon had a right to his moment of hubris. He and an associate, Allen Newell, brought to New Hampshire a computer that, history now shows, produced the most prominent research direction to emerge from the convention: a direction that would adversely affect artificial intelligence for years to come.

Called the Logic Theory Machine, Simon and Newell's computer did one thing well: it was able to prove the geometric theorems set forth in Whitehead and Russell's masterwork, *Principia Mathematica.* Moreover, it did so quicker than most mathematicians—and in at least two cases, its solutions were far more efficient and more creative than those reached by its human counterparts.

The Logic Theory Machine was clearly capable of solving problems based on high-level questions. But did it possess intelligence? Simon thought it did, primarily because he thought the human mind was merely a "logic machine" like the one he and Newell had built. Indeed, as he designed the Logic Theory Machine, Simon's respect for the human brain, in an important respect, decreased. In time he would come to define the brain's information processing abilities in terms usually reserved to describe a computer. "The metaphor I'd been using," Simon said, "of a mind as something that took some premises and ground them up and processed them into conclusions began to transform itself into a notion that a mind was something which took program inputs and data, had some processes which operated on the data and produced output."

Simon's point of view was not unusual. It fit well with the tenor of the time. The idea that the brain is essentially programmable like a computer was enjoying a spate of support among many psychologists, neuroscientists and computer designers. But under close examination this assumption proves unwarranted. In fact, it becomes clear from Simon's very own description of the functional underpinnings of the Logic Theory Machine—in his allegiance to raw data (and not the more powerful elements of cognition) as the sole input and output of the computer—that the device is quite limited with respect to intelligence. Despite its outward abilities, the Logic Theory Machine was about as smart as a warehouse and about as close to a model of the human brain as a machine that can scan one thousand words per minute. It was really no more than the most prodigious data manipulator than had ever before been created.

The type of programming used in the Logic Theory Machine is now derogatorily called, in artificial-intelligence circles, the brute-force method. It has as its basis the notion that if all the information necessary to reach a solution is crammed into a computer's memory, then the computer can, by sheer speed of searching through the data, appear to be thinking for itself. The computer rummages through its embedded data and pores over its thousands of facts in trial-and-error style—those that help solve the problem are retained, those that are irrelevant are discarded. Finally it reaches a conclusion or a solution based on the choicest information available in its memory. The computer during this process is like someone late for a dinner party searching anxiously and hastily through a drawer for the one black bow tie (relevant data), tossing out odd pieces of clothing (irrelevant data) in a helter-skelter fashion. The trouble with this method is that a complex problem can bog down even the fastest computer. If the human brain, which operates so much slower than a computer, functioned in this formalized "read everything" fashion, as Simon claimed it did, the movement of life would be reduced to a paralyzing snail's pace.

To illustrate how different human thinking is from the way the Logic Theory Machine worked, consider the following scenario and its solution: A man is told that if he gets to Atlantic City within two hours, he can claim one million dollars waiting for him at a blackjack table. Unconsciously, the man immediately separates the problem into what he knows and what he needs to know. For instance, he already knows (and intuitively knows that he knows) what Atlantic City is, how to get to there, what one million dollars is and why he would want to possess it. But he doesn't know (and must get answers from some outside source): what the plane schedule to Atlantic City is; at which blackjack table and casino the money is waiting; and how much the flight to Atlantic City costs and whether he has enough funds to cover the trip. In seconds, he will create a plan that defines the known, the unknown and how he intends to use both of them. What's more, this plan will be geared to achieving his goal: receiving one million dollars. Goal satisfaction is a central catalyst of human intelligence.

If, as the Logic Theory Machine would have, he had sorted through the amalgam of information stored in his memory one piece at a time, he'd have been frozen in place and would have surely lost the money. Fortunately, however, his mind does not work like the Logic Theory Machine. One important difference is that, as it takes in new information over a lifetime, the brain attaches to it what neuroscientists are now calling memory tags. Memory tags provide the brain with instant references to relevant data (not unlike an index) as needed. Also, internal pathways have evolved to retrieve that data efficiently. Trial-and-error and random searches are not commonly used by the human brain.

Clearly, then, there are stark differences between the mind and the Logic Theory Machine. Contrary to Simon's statements, his program deserved no real or metaphorical comparison with the human brain. But the program was hard to ignore because it solved mathematical theorems, a domain we have characterized as requiring intelligence to navigate. In truth, though, if the Logic Theory Machine were asked to answer a question of simple division, it would have confusedly stumbled through its thought processes and in many cases produced totally illogical answers. It had only high-level, preset and limited pathways of reasoning, based on high-level, preset information about mathematical theorems. The machine was inflexible and could not adjust to more mundane problems.

Unfortunately, this analysis of the Logic Theory Machine was never uttered at the 1956 Dartmouth conference. The masterful theorem-solving performance of the computer simply enchanted too many at the convention. The Logic Theory Machine seemed to be proof that the mind, indeed, might be modeled on a computer. Artiticial-intelligence researchers, at the time, were so eager to embrace the program that they never looked behind its curtain to uncover the legerdemain.

The sad fact is that, to put it bluntly, this one computer program set back the discipline by as many as twenty years. For as word of its exaggerated abilities spread throughout the fledgling artificial-intelligence community, imitations were spawned and proliferated. Gone for the time being was any attempt to design new models of the mind. Instead, creating machines that worked like the Logic Theory Machine took up almost everyone's time throughout the 1950s and most of the 1960s.

Machines based on the same brute-force programming and data-manipulation methods followed in droves. They were designed to be chess and checkers champions, mock psychiatrists and even electronic stock brokers. Joseph Weizenbaum, an MIT computer science professor and an artificial-intelligence researcher since the discipline's earliest days, has called these programs "computers in performance mode"; they merely imitate and mimic human cognition. Their output appears intelligent, but they do not offer a structural model of cognition.

Weizenbaum was speaking from intimate experience. He

was coauthor of one of the more well-known descendants of the Logic Theory Machine, ELIZA, which simulates conversation between a therapist and a patient. ELIZA at work looked like this:

ELIZA: Good afternoon, please type in your name.
Patient: John Atkins.
ELIZA: John, what brought you here today?
Patient: I'm feeling a bit sad.
ELIZA: Why are you sad?
Patient: I've been on the road a lot, and away from my family.
ELIZA: Tell me about your family.

If you look at the program's dialogue carefully, it becomes obvious that ELIZA is merely choosing the key words in the patient's statements—*sad* and *family* in this case—and attaching them to a programmed question format stored in the computer's memory. Almost as soon as he built ELIZA, Weizenbaum rejected the program vociferously as having no therapeutic value and being capable of nothing more than rote "cocktail party chatter." He labeled it a charade and an act of pure showmanship.

But others in artificial intelligence disagreed with his analysis. In effect, they refused to permit him to unmask the foolhardiness of the brute-force, Logic Theory Machine era of artificial-intelligence research. There were constant attempts to implement similar programs in a variety of settings; unfortunately, these programs proved to be as inflexible as the Logic Theory Machine.

The chess-playing programs that emerged in large numbers at that time were a good example. Most of these computers thought through their chess moves by a method that some have called *counting out*, that is, by considering every conceivable possibility on the board in brute-force programming fashion. One program, for instance, took fifteen minutes to analyze 26,000 alternative moves in a crucial game situation and still failed to reach the "correct" move arrived at by a grand master, who claimed, after introspection, to have considered only about one hundred moves. Clearly, in a game of chess, if every single branch of moves is to be thought through, alternatives multiply so quickly that the entire game becomes a process of paralyzingly slow analysis.

The programmers of that period did arrive at one theoretical solution to this problem: allow the computer to look at certain less common game pathways only occasionally. For instance, the machine was instructed not to search for move combinations that would lead to sacrificing its queen except in certain special circumstances. This programming solution failed principally because it was impossible to teach the computer when it was relevant to think of the queen sacrifice and when it was not in any reliable way. Narrowing down the search proved to be counterproductive in this case, and led to more erroneous moves than successful ones. The chess-playing computer needed the security of brute-force thinking to think well at all. Chess-playing programs, like the Logic Theory Machine, were utterly inflexible. They lacked perhaps the one essential ability that defines intelligence—the ability to home in immediately on the correct paths to reach a goal and, thus, to reserve one's knowledge to deal with the unexpected.

Ultimately, the Logic Theory Machine era ran its course. Almost all of the active researchers in artificial intelligence today have rejected the offspring of the 1956 convention. The emphasis in the discipline has changed so that now most of the researchers are far more interested in understanding specific, not general, human mental processes and in modeling them on a computer; they are far less interested in computers that replicate certain attributes of cognition on the outside, but on the inside show themselves to be mere pretenders.

"[A Logic Theory Machine era program] could prove a Euclidean theorem, but the machine could not understand what a triangle is in the many deep ways that a human being does," says Marvin Minsky, a professor of computer science at MIT and one of the attendees of the Dartmouth conference. "Perhaps the simplest problems, e.g. playing tic-tac-toe or proving the very simplest theorems of logic, can be solved by simple recursive application of all the available transformations to all the situations that occur. This becomes impractical in more complex problems as the search space grows larger and each trial becomes more expensive in time and effort."

Minsky's feelings about the early artificial-intelligence work are echoed by Roger Schank, chairman of the computer science department at Yale, and one of the more energetic and innovative artificial-intelligence researchers working today. "The problem is that what we have learned from the early research is only how to write programs that contain a fixed set of rules about a specific domain—be it mathematical theorems, chess playing, or medicine. And the computer, using its rules, in a rigid, formalistic way can solve some limited group of problems in these domains. But we haven't been able to write a program that can learn and teach itself how to form its own rules. There's a lot of hard stuff out there we just don't have the answers to. And that's the kind of work we should be spending our time on."

The "hard stuff" that Schank is referring to is bound up in some of the most tenacious questions facing artificial-intelligence researchers today: How do humans think? What are the goal-oriented pathways of intelligence that people commonly employ? How can intelligence in its fullest definition be transposed from an intangible process that humans possess genetically into a tangible, formalized and logical program that can run on a computer?

The work of the Logic Theory Machine era could have left artificial intelligence in ruins. But because people like Schank and Minsky and quite a few others have battered away at the discipline's failings, and have proposed more thoughtful, and successful, theories, the answers to these questions are finally beginning to appear closer than they once seemed.

# Chapter 2

# TURING'S FAILED LEGACY

The scientific philosophies supporting artificial intelligence evolved from the ideas of Alan M. Turing and his colleagues in computer design, who worked in the 1940s and early 1950s. For many years they were heroic figures in the discipline. Their analogy between the brain and the computer inspired the human-imitation and brute-force-programmed software of the late 1950s. But now, these men are treated far less reverentially by the artificial-intelligence community. Most of Turing's theories—and those of his associates—relating to artificial intelligence have been found to be severely flawed. Rejecting them, though, has been in itself an educational effort. Because in disproving Turing's ideas about the nature of machine intelligence, detail by detail, current artificial-intelligence researchers have built the underpinnings of their trade.

Alan Turing was an outspoken freethinker who made his mark originally as a mathematician while working in the grim laboratories of Cambridge University in prewar England. Turing's chief contribution to society was in breaking the code for the Enigma machine during World War II. The Enigma machine camouflaged German messages, and Turing's success at decoding these Axis strategy memos is now considered one of the keys that enabled the British to fend off Hitler's incursion.

His work as a military decoder brought Turing respect from his colleagues, but this failed to translate into large-scale government or scientific support for his research. His career was hampered by the fact that he was a homosexual, something that kept English politicians, guided by prejudice and the fear of adverse publicity, at arm's length. Thus, when the British government began to fund the more ambitious computer design projects in the period after the war, Turing was overlooked. A decade later, angry and frustrated, he took his own life.

But despite being less than popular among the powers-that-be throughout his career, Turing was always ambitious. He worked long hours, designing computers and investigating the concept of intelligent machines. Beginning in the 1930s, well before any computer hardware was operating, Turing described in treatises, and modeled on blueprint paper, machines that perfectly presaged the computer. These descriptions provoked long scholarly debates with colleagues during which they jousted over whether these computers, when fully developed, would be anything more than slaves of their data, whether they could ever possess human intelligence. Turing's position was clear on this. He never swayed from his conviction that artificial intelligence, in some form, would be a reality in the postwar decades.

Turing approached artificial intelligence by defining the similarities and dissimilarities, as he understood them, between the brain and the computer. He contended that if the way the brain functions could be broken down into its tiniest details, a model of it that simulated human intelligence skills could be fashioned on a computer. That contention itself was an achievement of high measure. Its purity of vision set a direct and uncompromising goal for artificial-intelligence research. Unfortunately, Turing was unable to take it any further. He was operating with a basic flaw that tainted all of his work in artificial intelligence: His knowledge of the brain was tragically naive and fundamentally ill-conceived. This doomed his research at its outset.

Turing's ideas concerning artificial intelligence were struck first and foremost a full ten years before a computer even arrived on the world scene. In a landmark paper written in 1935 called "Computable Numbers," Turing not only offered extensive details on how a computer could be designed and how it would operate, he also favorably likened his computer—the Turing machine, as he called it—to the human brain. Some in his time thought Turing eccentric, but very few in academia could ignore his pronouncements; consequently, "Computable Numbers" set a direction for thinking about computers, intelligence and the brain that would have to be reckoned with for years to come.

For computer designers, "Computable Numbers" was of inestimable value. The computer, Turing wrote, will be a machine that responds to precise instructions written in a logical order. In essence, Turing was describing binary programming, which is still the type of programming most computers operate with today. Simply put, a binary program—as Turing presented it and as it remains today—is a list of zeros and ones which the computer reads as prompts to alternately turn one of its circuits on or switch one off. Depending on the purpose of the program, the programmer's zeros and ones are translated by the computer into specific real-world actions. A series of binary code might cause a computer to say yes or no, paint black or white, move to stage two of the theorem or leap to stage 50 and so on. But, whatever action the computer takes, in all cases it is the result of a previous action. The computer "thinks" serially. It is a machine tied to sequential, logical reasoning.

Turing's was a well-thought-out portrait of a computing machine, one that in time proved to be accurate to an uncanny degree. Less accurate was his subsequent statement that to learn the way the Turing machine works is to understand the human brain. Still, because of Turing's academic reputation, the arguments in "Computable Numbers" enjoyed an excellent response. Because Turing tackled issues of neuroscience, computer design and mathematics in one paper, researchers in all of those fields looked at it very carefully. Neuroscientists, for instance, hoped to use Turing's brain/machine analysis as a way to further their knowledge about the mind; similarly, computer designers saw in it the indications they were hoping for that artificial intelligence can be created.

But the paper's essential flaw remained, and Turing was not entirely to blame for it. His ill-conceived description of the brain as a programmable machine was a reflection of the backward state in which mind research was bogged down at that time. Though researchers still are largely in the dark about the specific building blocks of human intelligence, over the past thirty years the amount of information uncovered makes what was known before 1950 a negligible muddle.

Turing, the colleagues whom he influenced and those who influenced him were all saddled with an image of the brain as a precise mechanistic organ, similar to a machine. This idea held sway during the first fifty years of the twentieth century, as landmark biological discoveries showed that most of the human body could be described in the same terms used to describe machines. (Many grammar school children, in fact, are still introduced to the body with an analogy to the automobile engine.) Thus, by extension, it was thought, wrongly, by most of the scientific and scholarly community during Turing's time that the brain could also be made to fit such an orderly, mechanical and convenient description. The consensus that emerged in that period was that the brain is a mosaic, with separate, localized and independent compartments exclusively responsible for each intelligence-based task.

The mosaic brain enjoyed wide circulation and was popular in publications of the time, from *Scientific American* to the *Encyclopedia Britannica.* Articles often contained illustrations depicting a cross-section of a human brain divided into any number of separate boxlike compartments. Each compartment was labeled with such arbitrary headings as memory, thought, intuition, vision and so on. Even love, hate and godliness sometimes merited a compartment. The conventional wisdom was that each complex human function resided in one of the sectors of the mosaic. Further, each sector barely communicated, if at all, with the others.

Though there was no scientific evidence for the mosaic-brain theory, it was hardy and endured. Indeed, as a result of Turing's comparison between the human brain and the computing machine, it became even more sharply defined. Noting that the computer was powered by discrete, self-contained electronic components, researchers conjectured that in a similar way, each series of nerve cells in the brain —each compartment in the mosaic—is a local power unto itself with its own separate and well-defined command structure.

This line of thought was particularly enticing to two American researchers, Warren McCulloch, a neurophysiologist from the University of Illinois Medical School, and his partner, Walter Pitts, a mathematician. In 1943, McCulloch and Pitts read Turing's "Computable Numbers" and wrote a paper that offered a strategy for building a computer-based model of the brain. They hypothesized that if purely electronic descriptions of brain cells and how they communicate with each other could be written, a task they thought simple, then by transferring these descriptions to the computer's circuitry an intelligent machine would result.

They added: "Because of the all-or-none character of nervous activity [in the brain], neural events and the relations among them can be treated by means of . . . logic." Clearly, they were borrowing freely from Turing's schema of binary programming. By describing the cells of the brain with phrases like "all-or-none character" and "treated by means of logic," McCulloch and Pitts were attributing the properties of a still-undeveloped electronic machine to the poorly understood human brain. This position was indefensible, lacking any proof, but it amassed its converts. Perhaps it was the powerful possibilities inherent in the position—chiefly, that here was a ready-made formula for replicating human intelligence—that served to make it so seductive.

One important convert who would vigorously enlist this brain/machine comparison in his research was W. R. Ashby, a respected British neurologist and a colleague of Turing's. Philosophically at least, the two men had a close relationship that was fostered by an interdisciplinary admiration for each other's work. In 1952, Ashby wrote a book, *Design for a Brain*, that could be called a bible for the Turing/McCulloch/Pitts/et al. point of view. In the preface, Ashby wrote: "This book has as basis . . . the hypothesis that [the nervous system] is essentially mechanistic. . . . We shall be dealing not with what an organism feels or thinks, but with what it does." Ashby considered the nervous system in its manifested behavior only—he assumed, essentially, that it has no philosophical underpinnings, just overt working parts. His goal was to begin the process of identifying the separate, discrete neural components that Turing and his colleagues required for the intelligent computer.

Ashby's book is filled with mechanical terms used to describe how the human mind works. Nerve cells are reduced to parameters, variables, critical component states, serial adaptation, feedback loops and the like. The last several chapters of the book are devoted to a mathematical explanation of the human brain, replete with graphs, charts and tables that Ashby divined by studying a primitive (and irrelevant) machine he built as a model of the brain.

Starting with the notion that the brain is an electro-mechanical organ, Ashby created a device to replicate it that had a magnet at its center. When Ashby shot electrical charges at it from varying angles, the magnet changed direction. Ashby leaped to the assumption that the way his device reacted to electrical prodding was a representation of the brain's responses to stimuli in its environment. Nerve cells, he was suggesting, are like blind sheep aimlessly following the lead of shifting electrical currents. And he used this misbegotten theory as the basis for his illustrative depictions of the human brain in his book.

Fortunately, no attempt was made to use Ashby's volume as a textbook for modeling the mind on the computer, for it would have led to a dead end. On the other hand, a good deal of hands-on (and ultimately misguided) research not directly related to Ashby's book grew out of similar comparisons between the brain and the machine that were then current. One case in point emerges in the 1949 correspondence between Turing and the British behavioral neurophysiologist, J. Z. Young.

Young was trying to quantify intelligence. To do this he assumed that the number of neurons in each compartment of the mosaic brain literally became larger as the function of the compartment became better defined in an individual's brain; that is, as the individual matured. Young had concluded from studies he performed that people "group their reactions [to their environment] around relatively simple models—circle, god, father, machine, state, etc." This theory, tied to Jungian psychology, said that people relate and respond to the world using these common "master" symbols. Further, Young felt that as people understood and felt more comfortable with these symbols they could be said to be growing more intelligent. Finally, Young assumed, with little reason, that this increased intelligence was accompanied by larger numbers of neurons in each of the relevant mosaic compartments of the brain. Essentially, Young's views were gathered from questionable psychological studies of behaviorism and intelligence; in a farfetched effort, he was attempting to prove them correct by postulating the growth of neurons in the brain.

In a letter, Young asked Turing whether in his work with intelligent-machine design he had been able to analyze this phenomenon on a machine. Could Turing provide a formal (mathematical) description of how the nerve cells in the brain's cortex evolved into thicker clusters as the human (or a machine) became more intelligent. He added that he felt it would be a great help if the connections between nerve cells and where they were aligned in the brain could be specified. "I feel," he said, "[this would allow us] to disentangle neural growth patterns somehow."

Turing, responding honestly, pleaded ignorance. He admitted that his knowledge was still very limited on this subject. "I am afraid," he wrote to Young, "I am very far from the stage where I feel inclined to start asking any anatomical questions. . . . That will not occur until quite a late stage when I have a fairly definite theory about how things are done."

Turing added, though, that he was attacking "anatomical

questions" by "working on a mathematical theory of embryology." This would be an all-consuming effort of Turing's and one that he spent long nights dickering with on one of the first computers, the Ferranti Mark I, in his offices at the Computing Laboratory of Manchester University. Turing was chronicling the shapes and growth patterns in plant leaves in hopes of devising equations that could quantify and predict how genetic organization is built in leaves. "Brain structure has to be one which can be achieved by the same genetical embryological mechanism," Turing said. He, like Young, felt that implicit in the brain's organization must be some combination of order, patterns and preordained designs.

Turing's research into plant genetics turned out to be a cul-de-sac as far as adding anything to artificial intelligence, brain modeling or even leaf embryology research. Looking at it in hindsight, it was a nearly impossible effort. We have since learned that, during brain development, there are close to 30,000 genes specific to the brain and involved in a veritable mountain of nearly untraceable activity; genes that, though we now have a library of genetic knowledge available, perform their complex jobs in a mysterious fashion, still undeciphered by humans.

Turing's argument that neurons and computer circuits are equatable lacked any scientific justification. Even so, he went on to a corollary that bore equal importance for artificial-intelligence research. This was the idea that the brain is programmable—that intelligence and knowledge in all their rich complexity could be packaged in a formal program.

Turing considered all human brains to be nothing but

homogeneous empty boxes of carefully ordered electronic circuitry waiting for data to manipulate. He argued that all individuals share common learning techniques; people do not design their own. Furthermore, the knowledge we take in is in the form of bulk precast information. If both the learning techniques and the knowledge base were encoded, he reasoned, they could be turned into a program that a computing machine could easily ingest and understand.

"The isolated man," Turing wrote, "does not develop any intellectual power. It is necessary for him to be immersed in an environment of other men, whose techniques he absorbs during the first twenty years of his life. He may then perhaps do a little research of his own and make a very few discoveries that are passed on to other men. From this point of view the search for new [learning] techniques must be regarded as carried out by the human community as a whole, rather than by individuals."

Turing was as off-base with this concept as he was with the nerve-cell-equals-computer-component idea. He badly underestimated the uniqueness of each individual's intelligence. Today, even after thirty years of artificial-intelligence research, identifying the subtle methods that each of us use as individuals to learn and acquire knowledge—and devise a common ground—still eludes the best efforts of those in the field.

Turing's lifetime of work in artificial intelligence, his misplaced emphasis on a mathematical model of the brain and his reliance on a too-simple analysis of knowledge and intelligence made him increasingly frustrated. So finally, in some desperation, he defined the one criterion for identifying intelligence in a machine that, he felt, could not be overpowered by subsequent research. Eventually known as the Turing test, his criterion stated that if a machine *appears* to think in human terms, then it does think. Put another way, if a human and a computer were hidden behind a curtain, and if an interrogator on the other side of the curtain, receiving written answers to questions about any subject from each, could not discern which was the machine and which the human, then the computer had passed the Turing test. Of course, to pass the test, the computer would have to possess enough intelligence to be cagey and not outshine the human in those areas where it clearly could, such as in making calculations involving large numbers. This is the lingering paradox of the Turing test: Even to imitate intelligence, a machine needs intelligence.

Viewed critically, this test is seen by some in artificial intelligence as the last-ditch attempt of a defeated researcher, as the portrait of a scientist trying to find a shortcut to a proof that has consistently eluded him. Turing anticipated that criticism would greet his test in a statement to reporters that contradicted many of the goals he worked for during his career: "I believe that in about fifty years time, it will be possible to program computers . . . to make them play the imitation game [or Turing test] so well that an average interrogator will not have more than seventy percent chance of making the right identification after five minutes of questioning. The original question, 'Can machines think?' I believe to be too meaningless to deserve discussion. Nevertheless I believe that at the end of the century the use of words . . . will have altered so much that one will be able to speak of a machine thinking without expecting to be contradicted."

The statement sounds almost Orwellian. No model of the brain will yet be created on a computer, he is saying, but by shifting the meaning of the words that define brain modeling, machine intelligence will seem to have occurred. This idea, though not acceptable in the pure sciences, left an indelible mark on artificial intelligence. This can be seen in the fact that the Dartmouth conferees—most of whom earned their academic spurs reading Turing—accepted the Logic Theory Machine, which satisfied many of the rules of the Turing test, as a thinking computer. Others who dismissed the devices in the Logic Theory Machine family offered the same terms of dismissal when they rejected the Turing test.

"Turing was essentially in performance mode," says Joseph Weizenbaum, the MIT professor. "He said basically that if a machine behaves and you can't tell from its behaving under some circumstances whether it's a machine or a human, then it's intelligent. There isn't the slightest hint here that the explanation of the machine's behavior is at the same time even remotely related to an explanation of human thought. That issue doesn't arise."

Turing's limitations as an artificial-intelligence theorist were never examined closely in his day. Now, Turing is spoken about with discretion in artificial-intelligence research circles. Many of the workers in the field today feel about Turing's work the way many psychologists feel about Freud's: They see it as having great insight and importance but failing in fundamental ways. Indeed, rebelling against Turing's theories has spurred a good deal of the important breakthroughs that artificial intelligence has produced over the past few years.

# Chapter 3

# THE SECOND WAVE

Those who first provided the theoretical muscle to reject Turing's ideas about the brain were the neuroscientists. During the 1950s, while artificial-intelligence researchers were plodding along the seemingly endless off-ramp they had chosen for their discipline, researchers probing the brain began a full-scale assault on Turing, Ashby, McCulloch, Pitts and others and their concepts of the mechanistic mind.

Since the 1950s, the neurosciences have provided the scene for a host of significant achievements. We now understand the brain, intelligence and psychological processes in ways that could not have been predicted only twenty years ago. Neuroscientific theories have blossomed from an increased knowledge of human cognitive skills. And these theories are at the heart of most of the important successes in artificial-intelligence research occurring today.

Turing's theories about the brain were the stuff of fantasy. They were borrowed from research—his own and others'—based on poorly gathered circumstantial evidence. The neuroscientists since Turing have not operated in a similar vacuum of misbegotten information. Their well-founded ideas have emerged from years of investigations probing people's behavior and thought processes, as well as actual observation and mapping of neural activity in the brain as seen through the most powerful electronic microscopes.

Looking at it from the broadest perspective, the wholesale change in the way we think about the brain that has occurred since the 1940s has been brought about by the downfall of the concept of the mind as mosaic. We now know that the brain is organized not as a localized, compartmentalized system, but as a distributive system. And although the brain apparently does have numerous specialized modules that might be considered separate compartments, carefully garnered evidence reveals that these modules are interconnected with—not separated from—each other in complex ways.

Far from being entirely separate entities, as the mosaic would imply, many of the brain's large, specialized modules have sections that are physiologically alike. In fact, these sections are formed by the continuous replication of absolutely identical cellular units. Because of this, single brain events can occur in different specialized modules simultaneously; they simply occur in the otherwise identical sections of the separate specialized modules. In this way, the brain apparently performs tasks redundantly. In effect, each separate module is not limited to entirely distinct jobs, but is able to perform some of the same functions as its companion modules.

Gary Lynch, a forty-year-old professor neurobiology at the University of California at Irvine, studies the way humans form and retain memories. In doing so, he has observed a fascinating example of this interdependency of brain parts, which occurs between the huge outer layer, the cerebral cortex, and the hippocampus, a tiny, fingerlike structure located in the secondary layer. "If you take . . . the hippocampus," Lynch says, "and put electricity through it, just bip! literally that long, the [definitions] of the nerve circuits [in the hippocampus] change and don't go back. . . . Now those same changes, we have found, occur in the cerebral cortex, too, at the same time. This despite the fact that the cerebral cortex is not hit by any electricity. . . . In both regions, the physical change in the circuit can last for weeks or months or longer."

What's more, each section of a brain module is not necessarily linked to all of the other sections in that module, but, interestingly, each is linked to similarly segregated subsets in other modules. In short, unlike a mosaic, the brain is an organ with widespread redundancy throughout all its large modules, an organ that can, flexibly, redefine itself as the body requires. This redundancy would explain, for instance, how, if one-half of the brain is destroyed, even in the area where memory resides, the brain still does not necessarily lose all of its stored thoughts.

Perhaps the first major explorer of the brain to see its intertwined nature in a holistic way was Vernon B. Mountcastle, a professor of neurosciences at Johns Hopkins University, who was cited in 1983 when he won the coveted

Lasker Award for being "the first investigator" to go beyond the simple observation, description and classification of brain function to ask the fundamental question: "How does the brain, as a whole, process the information the senses gather?" Mountcastle and his colleagues in Baltimore have watched biological secrets unravel, and ultimately have been given a view of the order and the structure of individual nerve cells, an accomplishment without equal.

Mountcastle's work irrevocably puts to rest any vestige of the concept of the brain as a localized mosaic. "The brain is much more of a unit," Mountcastle says. "It is far more integrative than hierarchical [as the mosaic would claim]. The idea of a hierarchy, the idea of local areas giving commands, no. Impossible." And in a direct, though not necessarily intended, swipe at the McCulloch/Pitts contention that a graphically depicted portrayal of the "all-or-none" character of specific nerve cells could be used as a pattern for an intelligent computer, Mountcastle adds: "The principles of [individual] cell biology . . . are . . . not sufficient to form ordering rules for the function of large numbered systems like the cerebral cortex. The ensemble properties of those populations [of cells contained in the cortex] are not directly predictable by summing the properties of individual cells."

The work of Mountcastle and his colleagues has precipitated a move by other neuroscientists and artificial-intelligence researchers away from viewing the brain in terms of its most infinitesimal components and then comparing it to the computing machine. Instead, many researchers now insist that the brain must be viewed as a total system, as an organ with a unique structural design, not merely as a collection of individual nerve cells. Indeed, even beyond the debunking of the mosaic mind, what becomes clear the more one looks at the brain and compares it to the computer is that, despite Turing's contention, very few similarities exist. In many ways the brain pales as a mechanistic and efficient machine next to the computer; but the computer falls equally short in its ability to creatively shape information until it can be called knowledge.

Some basic facts emerge when the brain and the computer are analyzed side by side. First, the computer is a carefully regulated machine, usually fueled by a master clock, that performs its operations in utter synchronicity; the brain is notoriously asynchronous. Second, the computer handles data at the speed of light, with the latest circuitry executing five million instructions per second; the brain's components are extremely slow by comparison—nerve impulses travel at only two to three hundred feet per second. Third, the computer can easily juggle numbers so complex that they may contain as many as twelve digits; the brain of even the smartest math genius can only manipulate numbers that are made up of, at most, three digits. Fourth, the computer keeps its data in distinct and separate internal mailboxes; the brain, on the other hand, has an extremely nonlocal and nonlinear information-access structure that distributes its stored data throughout the organ. Finally, if one percent of the transistors in a computer fail, the computer locks up, unable to proceed; the brain is far more robust and can continue working capably even if it loses one-half of its "moving parts."

Perhaps the most overriding difference between the

brain and the computer is evident in the complete flexibility of the human mind. While the computer relies on strictly programmed instructions that it chains through in a carefully diagrammed fashion to reach a decision or a solution, the brain operates off of a mutative and pliant relationship among its neurons. A traditional computer can be described as "hard wired" in that every programming instruction and interaction in its operating system follows a predictable and unchangeable path to a conclusion; the brain is, by comparison, wedded to plasticity. This utter flexibility allows the human being to fluidly change direction and immediately chart correct courses despite the changing pace of events around him.

"If you want to compare it to a computer the only way to describe the brain is that while in some sense it is indeed hard wired, its very circuitry is able to change automatically to any given signal," says Gary Lynch of the University of California. "In thirty milliseconds, a time frame we cannot imagine, you can take sluggish communication between two cells and sharpen it to the point where they will respond to each other distinctly every single time a message is sent."

Indeed, the relationship among nerve cells in the brain is underlined by the fact that in any given instance each nerve cell—and how it reacts to neighboring cells—is wholly unpredictable. Every neuron can hold a different amount of a chemically based transmission substance in its vesicles or nerve-ending sacs before a threshold level is reached; at the threshold level, the vesicles' contents must be fired to the next neuron. However, if the receiver neuron has a higher threshold than the transmitting cell, the information being sent may be rejected. Moreover, a message may even be passed back to the transmitting neuron that it ought to inhibit its zeal to communicate in the future. But, as Lynch pointed out, each neuron-to-neuron chemical transmission is capable of shifting at any given instant.

One British biochemist, Steven Rose, has taken this a step further and actually diagrammed the nature of neuron-to-neuron communications. Rose states that there are three types of events that cause the release of chemical packets across the synapses between neurons. Only one is absolutely formal and predictable. The predictable neuronal exchanges—where nerve cells must exchange information—are the result of either messages that arrive from some external source in the outside world (heat, fear of an imminent attack, an emotional reaction) or messages that the body itself initiates voluntarily or involuntarily (a hand movement, a heartbeat). Of the other two types of events that cause neurons to release chemical packets, one is largely predictable, as in the firing of a neuron because it has reached a threshold level. The other is always random, as in the unexpected and extemporaneous release of chemicals across the synapse. As Rose explains: "At the synapses between cells lies the choice point which converts the human nervous system from a certain, predictable and dull one into an uncertain, probabilistic and interesting one. It is not too strong to say that the evolution of humanity followed the evolution of the synapse."

Clearly, this is a bold statement that totally lays to rest the all-or-none mechanistic description of the brain so prevalent in the 1940s and early 1950s. Through all of this, what has been learned is that the computer and the brain are really two entirely diverse creations; one is stolid, the other is animated; one is programmable, the other defies formalities. Pure design transference will simply not yield humanlike intelligence in a machine.

It has been a long road, but all of the work in neuroscience has finally persuaded artificial-intelligence researchers to dismiss descriptions of the brain as a totally efficient machine, descriptions such as those Turing and his followers tried to shove into the formal logic of the computer as one would shove a misfit into a straitjacket. Taking their place is the realization that if the way the brain works is to be modeled on a machine, the model will have to be based upon exceptionally well-designed views of human intelligence and how knowledge is processed, and not on component or engineering theories.

Consequently, one of the central lines of investigation into artificial intelligence currently being pursued involves intricate analysis of how intelligence and learning are achieved. The eventual aim is to be able to encode in programs flexibility of thought, inferential procedures, rules of thumb and so on. Raw-data and brute-force programming are no longer the keys to an artificial-intelligence program; instead, the focus is on the more powerful and subtle knowledge and learning strategies people commonly use. Today's more complex attempts in the laboratory are still in their early stages. But already our ability to decipher and then program human cognitive processes is growing by unexpected leaps, paralleling the impressive neurological and cognitive work that led the way.

Ernest Kent, one of the most intuitive artificial-intelligence researchers today, provides a perfect example of the new direction in the discipline. Though he is only in his thirties, Kent combines the hybrid experience—he is part neuroscientist and part computer engineer—that now marks many of the basic researchers in artificial intelligence. Kent is a former professor of physiological psychology who now works for the federal government on a robotics project in which he is investigating human vision.

His academic resume is a whirlwind of activity. "I initially did a little undergrad work in physics but got my bachelors in biology with a lot of electives in psychology. My doctorate was in biopsychology where you have to fulfill all the requirements for a PhD in both biology and psychology. Then I took a job in physiological psychology which tries to explain behavior on the basis of neural function. I just always had a flair for electronics and machinery. In the course of running my experiments I needed to design and build a lot of electronic equipment. . . . I had to learn how to program computers and then, because funds in my school were limited, I had to learn how to repair them. So I've designed and built a lot of computers since about 1963, but I've never actually had a course in them."

In comparing the brain to a machine, Kent says that there is a simple difference between the two: "The brain finds adequate solutions to complex problems as opposed to exact solutions to simpler ones the way a computer does." This is not a facile statement. It points to an essential dichotomy between mind and machine that is now at the heart of artificial-intelligence work. And understanding how the brain is so uncannily efficient in nearly always arriving at the "adequate solution" will mark an important step toward modeling it on a computer.

Kent adds: "To create artificial intelligence you have to start by understanding the human problem you want to transfer to a computer. Then you have to define the cognitive functions involved in that problem." This line of reasoning, defining each individual segment of the cognitive process, has led researchers to study in depth the paramount tool that people use for intelligence and learning: heuristics. Today, nearly all artificial-intelligence research and design is linked closely to an examination of heuristic strategies used by people.

Heuristics, as understood in relation to artificial intelligence, are the internal strategies and common methods that humans use to solve problems. A heuristic is the specific, step-by-step thought process we rely on to go from Point A to Point B. Included in the heuristic are rules of thumb acquired through experience, educated guesswork about the plausible answer to a problem and the integration in diverse ways of our many knowledge-manipulation capabilities. To provide a simple example: Heuristics are at the heart of our thinking when we conclude, without consciously dredging up historical data stored in our memories, that if it's before seven in the morning, daily traffic patterns suggest that it would be wise to use Route 1; similarly, if it's been raining hard, road conditions make Route 2 the wise alternative.

"When humans attempt to solve a problem," Kent explains, "and they develop a heuristic to do it, it does not mean they have come up with a solution in the sense that there is an equation available to give us the correct result or that there is a specific algorithm to use. It means we have set up a pathway to search for the solution and make intermediate decisions."

Reaching a goal by using heuristics is an interdisciplinary activity in the human mind. The brain apparently subdivides the problem and searches throughout its breadth for all kinds of data—some of it to be rejected, some to be embraced, all to be held up against the projected goal to determine its worth. "If the goal is 'I want something to eat,'" Kent continues, "there are a lot of intermediate steps that the brain has to go through before it chooses what to eat and where to find it. The statement of the goal will come from the frontal lobes of the cerebral cortex. Then the visual cortex will provide the data of what kind of food is available and present some solutions for the goal. Perhaps, after looking through one's refrigerator, 'I want something to eat' will be changed to 'I want an apple.' If this is approved, the basal ganglia on the motor level may reach for the apple. But in addition, along the way, there are massive connections between the cortex and parts of the limbic system [the emotions] which lie beneath and may offset the decision."

Decisions in the making are constantly in flux because while the brain is settling on which final path to take—and in this case it may be to bite into the apple, to open the refrigerator, to prepare a meal or to go to the supermarket for food—we continually monitor floods of new sensory input. Any of this subsequent sensory input can be instrumental in changing our choice of paths used to reach a goal.

For instance, you may decide to satisfy the goal of appeasing your hunger by eating an apple. But as more data continues to reach the brain—even as the apple is about to be bitten into—you might switch gears (a moment of the inimitable human cognitive flexibility) in response to the thought: "I've just been to the dentist. Perhaps I better have a banana." You put the apple down, and pick up the banana.

Each heuristic is an entity unto itself. Each one is also a remarkable series of specific mental strategies. Thus, the well-chosen heuristic represents a diligent attempt to integrate, compare, and analyze a bombardment of data to produce a conclusion.

A concrete example of how research into heuristics applies to artificial intelligence is provided in Ernest Kent's own work, which breaks difficult ground in a most tenacious sector of artificial intelligence: vision and perception. Essentially he seeks to untangle the mysteries of visual heuristics—our strategies and mental skills of seeing, how we identify and understand the meaning of objects in our environment. Kent's goal is to fully understand the way the brain processes visual images and how these images are used when we make decisions and reach conclusions.

Although many are attempting to teach computers to see (see Chapter 6), Kent's research is unique. While others are content with modeling on computers small components of the human visual system, Kent is replicating human vision in its entirety. To do this he is using a computer to design the actual image-processing physiological and intellectual hierarchy he is convinced people rely on to see. Kent aims to culminate his work in a theory that demonstrates the way people identify and organize visual data; i.e., how we first name an object, then ascertain its importance based on past experience and finally conclude whether any other part of the body is required to interact with the object being looked at.

Kent's research is carried out in a tiny office located fifteen miles from Washington, D.C., in one of those countryside industrial parks that pepper the outskirts of metropolitan areas. His cramped space is made even more so by the boards of computer circuits stacked unceremoniously on chairs, the cluttered mishmash of flowcharts adorning the blackboard and the farrago of books, from Gray's *Anatomy* to texts on computer architecture and design, that lie pell-mell on the bookshelves. Incipient claustrophobia is relieved only by the view of a vast lawn encircled by distant pine trees which can be seen through a large window over Kent's desk.

Perhaps emphasizing his faithfulness to the basic-research branch of artificial intelligence, pictures of spiritual kin from earlier times and other disciplines, among them Bertrand Russell and Isaac Newton, hang prominently on his walls. Notably absent from this gallery are photos of Alan Turing and his colleagues, who would have liked to claim positions as the philosophical forebears of artificial intelligence.

When asked to describe the assumptions that form the foundation of his research, Kent offers a simple explanation: "I am not going to suggest," he says, "that we try to build a hardware replica of the brain, because we have neither the knowledge nor the hardware. . . . Instead, [I am going to] try to identify the principles of brain operation that can eventually be put to good use with the kinds of hardware that we do have."

Kent's work in general has been inspired by the pioneering brain research of Vernon Mountcastle. In particular as well, in his attempts to transfer the architecture of vision from the mind onto the computer, he has borrowed a central conclusion of Mountcastle's. Since the mid-1970s, Mountcastle and his colleagues at Baltimore's Johns Hopkins Hospital have spent long, tedious hours examining and then reconstructing under electron microscopes the precise alignment of neurons in the brain. They determined, in an unparalleled breakthrough, that the billions of nerve cells in the cerebral cortex are arranged in vertical columns rather than in a more circular and random mass, as was previously thought. This columnar architecture enables the brain to process and reprocess information in an exceedingly efficient and strategic order.

Kent brilliantly extrapolated a working design from Mountcastle's notion of neural organization and created what he calls the pipelined-image-processing device. Basically, this is a program whose "data cruncher" is divided into eight separate vertical compartments that emulate the columnar structure of nerve cells in the human brain. A visual image, perhaps a square, a circle or even a tree, focused on by the computer's video camera, travels through the eight compartments, stopping at each compartment for a different form of processing.

Before an image is delivered to the program's compartments, it is first transposed into digital data that the computer can understand. After being digitized, an image's data move in three separate directions as they flow through the eight compartments. First, the data travel in a forward pathway and are interpreted separately by each compartment. The initial box simply looks at the image; the next box determines the intersection of the edges within it; the third box "feels" the overall shape of each object in the image; the fourth box identifies their textures; the next box ascertains the image's 3-D spatial arrangement, and so forth. The results of each of these examinations are left behind and stored in each compartment as well as carried with the image as it makes its way through the column. By retaining data about visual images, each compartment is able to build a warehouse of memories with which to interpret subsequent images.

Second, the visual data travel in a retrograde pathway. As an image leaves a compartment, a copy of it returns to the beginning of that compartment for a second pass through it, essentially for secondary processing. This is an important aspect of Kent's work that illustrates how current artificial-intelligence research has squarely renounced earlier thinking in the field. By endorsing redundancy, or multiple passes, something accepted now by neuroscientists as a routine method the human brain uses to ensure efficient processing of information and memory storage throughout the organ, Kent has separated his view of the mind from the localized, nonredundant mosaic formerly in vogue in Turing's day. In Kent's computer, as in the brain, redundancy assures that each compartment does not ignore even the most subtle gradients of the visual image.

Finally, the visual data proceed in a recursive pathway. Each image, after being processed in all eight compartments, is returned to the first compartment. This time, though, the originally unidentified image carries with it a name tag, the result of its being examined closely by each of the eight compartments. And with the now-identified image back at the start of the loop, the computer uses what it has learned about the image to make decisions about it.

The compartments employ a simple process to identify images they receive from the video camera: they compare them to models of previously seen and identified images stored in their memories. For instance, having previously elicited all of the properties of a rectangle, they would tag a new image as a rectangle if it adequately fit their retained memories of that shape.

Unlike Newell and Simon's Logic Theory Machine, this computer's data base is made up both of information originally programmed into it and whatever it subsequently learns. Indeed, the fact that it has the ability to learn sets Kent's computer—and his work—apart from almost all vision research. His program is able to take an image it cannot identify and, based on new data it acquires, attach it to an image stored in memory to which it is most similar. And in modeling this mental process of comparing fresh and unknown images with ones that are familiar, Kent is replicating on a computer a common visual heuristic learning strategy.

For a simple example of this heuristic in use, assume that the computer knows from previous experience what a rectangle looks like. The first time it sees a square it would guess, from its properties, that it is merely a rectangle and not a unique shape. This is a correct assumption, of course, but only a partially correct one. As succeeding squares work their way through the computer, the machine will begin to realize that this is a separate type of rectangle, and ultimately the model of the square will reside in its memory as an entirely different image, one that has its own identity. In this way, the computer has actually widened its own understanding and taught itself a new concept about geometrical shapes.

Kent's computer is flexible enough to hold on to and periodically reexamine its temporary ideas about what an image is until it feels certain its conclusions are correct. Surely there is a margin for error in this process. But as is the case with the human brain—because the road to a specific solution is paved with the general rules of thumb that are the hallmark of heuristics—most of the time it should be accurate.

Kent's work is in its early stages. At this point, his computer is only able to make rudimentary visual identifications and even more primitive analyses of situations based on that data. For instance, most of the time it correctly names the shape it is looking at—even if it is camouflaged by surrounding objects. It is also able to execute simple commands, such as to move a circular object into a nearby rectangle. Obviously, with those limited abilities, the pipelined-image computer is no more intelligent than a two-year-old. Yet the computer is attempting a very subtle self-teaching process using important aspects of human visual heuristics. This could, in time, enable it to grow more knowledgeable as it sees and processes ever more complicated objects.

"The real power of this system," Kent says, "is that it can compare projected states with temporarily defined states." The projected state is the ultimate goal. The computer, for example, might be told to distinguish a square with nine-inch sides from a group of shapes. Temporarily defined states are those intermediate decisions that have to be made—Does the shape I am looking at have four equal sides? Are its sides each nine inches long?—before a correct answer can be found. As Kent sees it, learning and intelligence are the result of moving and combining small, unconnected pieces of knowledge—this object has four sides, each nine inches long (the temporarily defined states)—until they add up to a conclusion—the object is a square (the projected state).

While Kent is making only slow, incremental progress toward a fully formed intelligent machine, he has already succeeded in satisfying one of the central motives for his research: describing certain basic human intelligence processes. He has pinpointed an elusive clue through his program that suggests how the human brain physically processes information, something about which neuroscientists and artificial-intelligence researchers have long been in a quandary. Namely, does the brain process information in serial steps, one piece at a time, or does it process parallel chunks, looking at numerous slices of data simultaneously?

During Turing's reign the brain was thought to be a serial and discrete data manipulator, like a traditional computer. Then, because the brain refused to fit this mold, the pendulum swung the other way and it was assumed to be a parallel-processing organ. Kent's work lends itself to the conclusion that the brain employs a combination of the two processes. Kent's computer views images both serially—the visual data travel step by step, one piece following another—and also in a parallel fashion—the visual data are simultaneously being reanalyzed in recursive, or retrograde fashion even as they are moving forward.

Kent's research promises, in the long run, to offer a comprehensive structural model of human intelligence and a better understanding of how heuristics work. Even though vision research is one of the most difficult to tame of the branches of artificial intelligence, he is, at least, making a modicum of headway. What makes his work somewhat more apt to succeed in the short run is that he is currently investigating only geometrical shapes in the hope of applying machine understanding of shapes to real-world situations, such as factory design and automation and computer-based strategic defense.

But in a more general sense, Kent's work has already made a deep impact. By offering even a limited example of the heuristics of sight—especially the visual strategy that says that in seeing we build upon what we know to better understand what we are less familiar with—Kent is making an irrefutable case for the importance of heuristics in artificial intelligence. Moreover, he successfully exemplifies why artificial intelligence has now come full circle, from the enthusiastic promise of the 1940s and early 1950s to the failures of the next two decades to enthusiastic promise again today. His work proves that studying the human being as a thinking machine, rather than fruitlessly searching for mathematics, algorithms, components and variables in the brain, gives the discipline a sturdy hook on which to hang its theories.

One result of this new shift toward optimism is unalterably clear: The discipline's leading lights are not alone and unknown anymore as were the two dozen 1956 Dartmouth conference attendees. Now, two to three thousand participants, including the national media, gather in hotels such as the Washington Hilton for six-day events, replete with demonstrations of the latest in computer design from the country's largest high-tech firms and academic centers.

Included in this outpouring of interest in artificial intelligence are major articles on the subject in *Business Week*, *The New York Times*, *Newsweek* and other publications, which have lacked substance, but have convinced segments of the public that machine intelligence, in full scope, has arrived. Since artificial-intelligence propagandists have been hyping that claim for over thirty years, it is necessary to put a skeptical ear to the tracks. One thing is certain, however: AI researchers are beginning to revel in their press clippings. The official bumper sticker at the annual convention in Washington in 1983 read, "It's for real."

Is it? The answer is the same as it has been for three decades: no, not yet. But now there is a discernible change in the air—despite the flaunting tone of the bumper sticker. Scientists working in artificial intelligence are extremely serious about understanding the way people think. They realize that the time for technological razzle-dazzle, for machines that only appear to possess intelligence, is over for good.

Though artifical-intelligence researchers argue over certain technological specifics involved in teaching computers to think, all are faithful to the cause of rejecting the first wave of the discipline's research and replacing it with practical results. To this end, an ambitious agenda for artificial intelligence using a host of completely new technologies has emerged.

The most prominent form of artificial intelligence today is the expert system. The expert system is a computer that possesses the knowledge and some of the common-sense rules of an expert in a given field. It is thus able to arrive at original and intelligence-based solutions to problems in its domain, be it medicine, prospecting for minerals, diesel-engine repair, chemical molecular analysis or the design of computer circuits. This is because the expert system shares with humans the power to understand and alter symbols, concepts and numbers to provide solutions.

Expert-system technology is by far the most successful application of artificial intelligence to date, with over a dozen such computers operating in tandem with humans in hospitals, geological sites and laboratories, each of them proving to be at least as intelligent as the best of their human partners and significantly more gifted than their more mediocre counterparts. Priming the emergence of expert systems are the nearly one dozen firms—most of them founded by former artificial-intelligence academicians—that are designing and manufacturing them for commercial use. Expert systems are a growing American cottage industry, which by all estimates will produce sales in the multibillion-dollar range by 1990.

Expert systems do, however, have one obvious failing. They cannot understand the natural languages of people. This can make them especially difficult to use and communicate with unless you are nearly an expert in the field yourself. Expert systems gather information from their human counterparts with questions that can only be answered with a one-word, strictly formal response, or with numerical data. A computer that advises on the proper methods of oil drilling on rigs, for instance, might ask its colleague a question like this:

From a range of $-5$ to $+5$ what is the chance of interbedded shale at this site?

Attempting to communicate the nature of a physical environment by attaching an arbitrary number to one of its properties opens up the potential for erroneous subjective determinations by the human who inputs the data and inaccurate conclusions by the computer. To avoid this, a large branch of artificial-intelligence research is devoted to the second technology in the field: teaching the computer the English language, or what is called natural-language research. The ultimate aim is to allow the expert system and the computer user to have a conversation like this:

Computer: Describe the site and any problems you are encountering.
User: The site has interbedded shale that starts at 2,009 meters and goes down as deep as 3,695 meters. Below that is homogeneous shale that extends 3,716 meters below the surface. The drilling rig is sticking at about 2,695 meters.
Computer: To solve the problem you should circulate the mud with a normal flow. During circulation you should add lubricants.

Currently, this dialogue is not yet within any computer's capabilities. The machine simply cannot understand its human colleague's answer. Those three sentences are too full of complicated syntax and linguistic patterns that are literally child's play for people, but over the head of a computer.

There is one recently designed and operating artificial-intelligence-based system called Explorer that contains a data base of oil wells and can create sophisticated maps in response to human requests such as, "Show me a map of all tight wells drilled before May 1, 1980, but since May 1, 1970, by Texaco that show oil deeper than 2,000 feet, are themselves deeper than 5,000 feet, and are now operated by Shell." But the logical, predictable and structured nature of that sentence is far simpler for a computer to understand than the more freewheeling and random response that the user gave in the initial example. Though Explorer appears impressive, it is in reality using one of the earliest methods developed for teaching computers to comprehend natural language, a method that actually came out of the 1956 Dartmouth conference.

Originally, artificial-intelligence researchers thought they could succeed by programming into the computer a set grammatical path that would enable it to understand the structure of all sentences, similar to old-fashioned diagramming. Although mostly discredited today, this method is used in Explorer. The computer searches for key words—objects and subjects—in a sentence and attaches them to the loose verbs. It then reaches into its dictionary of probable words it will encounter, and by pulling the words' definitions and usages from the dictionary, the computer constructs the meaning of a sentence.

This is a useful approach as long as a sentence does not employ a word in a fashion that the computer's dictionary is not equipped to handle. For instance, if the human asked the computer to "Show me a map of all the tight wells drilled before the opening of the longest running Broadway show," the computer would be unable to react, stricken by its ignorance; it understands "show" as a verb, not as a noun. For the diagramming method to work, then, bigger and bigger dictionaries would constantly have to be devised, something that would both tax the memory of the computer and slow it down considerably as well. Moreover, in terms of artificial intelligence, even if a computer possessed an immense amount of words in its dictionary, it would still be nothing more than a dumb machine with a huge data base, totally unable to build its own language understanding.

Because of this, the diagramming method has been rejected as a useful method for maintaining a continuous dialogue between a computer and a human. To accomplish that, leading natural-language researchers, led by Roger Schank at Yale, assert that the computer will literally have to understand the meaning of each sentence, not just its structure. Schank, who is busy forging a neomodern linguistic theory, claims that we comprehend sentences not because of definitions or the grammatical placement of words, but because we intuitively "feel" the meaning of sentences. Ultimately, says Schank, computers must comprehend language in the same way.

People are able to understand that separate sentences often carry the same meaning, even if by defining them word by word the sentences seem to be disparate. To illustrate, people intuitively relate the statements "I like books" and "I like reading" by what Schank calls their conceptual meanings, not by their individual words. Broken down respectively into their three words, the first sentence would seem to indicate affection for an object and the second sentence affection for an action. Yet there is no doubt when hearing these sentences—or even much more complex and conceptually related ones—that they essentially mean the same thing. Similarly, if someone tells us "I like zucchini," we understand that the speaker eats the vegetable, though the action of eating is not specifically mentioned. Transferring this notion of conceptual meaning to artificial intelligence and onto machines is the focus of much of the current natural-language experimentation.

This work is beginning to produce results that will, over the next decade, lead to the development of expert systems that can converse in ordinary English; computers that can read huge amounts of information, summarize it and then offer strategic choices for action (this is especially important for corporate and military uses); translations systems that can offer simple explanations of technical manuals and decode foreign documents; and computers that can understand speech—not keyboard—input.

Perhaps more importantly, work in this branch of artificial intelligence is helping us, as Schank says, "through the use of computer models to discover how the human mind works and how it interprets language. Whatever commercial applications come from artificial-intelligence work, it is the fascination of studying human thought and cognition itself that makes the discipline so significant."

Expert systems and computers that understand at least

simple language have come a long way in a few short years. They far surpass in potential applications the work being done in the third new technology embraced by artificial-intelligence researchers: the creation of smart robots. Still, though it is the least advanced branch in the field, robotics is perhaps the most significant. This is because the design of cognitive-based robots combines the attributes of expert systems and natural-language comprehension with one other human capability: vision.

An artificially intelligent robot would have extensive knowledge of particularly taxing subjects, such as industrial design or military strategy; be able to accept human input and offer advice in the natural words of its human interrogator; and "see," mostly through laser or video eyes, the environment it is operating in—all of this in order to make decisions as to the correct next move for its mechanical limbs. In short, the intelligent robot would be a machine that has integrated three important human senses.

Potentially, the use of robots can free humans from working in toxic industrial situations, such as nuclear-waste clean-up sites, and from serving on the assembly line. The robot will do the most tedious and arduous jobs, as well as handle some of the most difficult decision making. Robotic factory foremen, so the plan goes, will minimize inventory and production bottlenecks. Fluctuations in orders and supplies of raw materials needed for construction as well as tooling breakdowns can be automatically addressed by robots who will take responsibility for shifting production schedules. Experts estimate that the advent of smart robots will enable factories to cut inventories by five percent and improve productivity by as much as 20 percent. In addition, the Pentagon intends to create robotic weapons, such as unmanned submarines, drone aircraft and powerful land vehicles that combine artifical intelligence with high-powered computing. Admittedly, today's robots offer far more in the way of brawn than brains, but the keen interest in these machines shown by both industry and the military is expected to propel this fledgling branch of artificial intelligence into the mainstream.

The three major branches of artificial-intelligence research—expert systems, natural languages, and robotics—would be merely interesting offshoot theories not deserving of a second glance were it not for the strong financial support they enjoy. Indeed, one of the strongest indications that artificial intelligence is for real this time, as the bumper sticker proclaimed, lies in the fact that the most important tiers of the American technological community are committed to it in a big way. Foremost, in terms of dollars, is the military, which is licking its lips at the prospect of intelligent computer-aided defense. A 1981 study by the Defense Science Board, conducted as the Reagan administration defense buildup began, ranked artificial intelligence in the top ten of military technologies necessary for maintaining an adequate defense posture during the 1980s. On the basis of this report, the Pentagon is requesting slightly over $1 billion through 1986 specifically for artificial-intelligence research.

Separate from the mainstream Pentagon channels is the Defense Advanced Research Projects Agency (DARPA), which has sponsored most of the major technological breakthroughs in telecommunications and computers over the last thirty years. DARPA is gazing longingly at artificial intelligence as well and is already spending $100 million annually on research.

Ranking just below the military in the amount of money spent, corporate America is pouring its resources into artificial intelligence. All of the major high-tech powerhouses are earmarking substantial sums—in many cases over $2 million annually—for artificial-intelligence-systems research and design. Every familiar, innovative American corporation is jockeying to be a leader in expert systems, natural language or robotics advances.

Perhaps the most unique of the corporate artificial-intelligence ventures is a recently formed consortium called the Microelectronics and Computer Technology Corporation (MCC). MCC is a partnership of twelve battle-weary competitors in the computer field, including Honeywell, Motorola, RCA and Control Data. The companies donate scientists and researchers to work exclusively for MCC for up to four years and put up the money to fund the consortium's advanced computer research. In return, member firms have the right to use MCC's research in future designs. MCC's budget, supporting a staff of 250, is $75 million a year.

The final tier of the current American artificial-intelligence effort is based in the same university centers that spawned the discipline—chiefly Yale, Carnegie-Mellon, Stanford, Dartmouth and the Massachusetts Institute of Technology. In 1956, artificial-intelligence researchers from these schools were consigned to roughhewn laboratories in the most forgotten corners of the universities; the feeling among many was that the discipline would probably fade away from a lack of success. But today, despite its somewhat checkered record, artificial-intelligence departments with the most modern equipment and comfortable surroundings are common at all of these schools and many others.

Moreover, the academic arena has spawned a growing number of start-up corporations, founded by leading university artificial-intelligence researchers. These companies are designing commercially available computers with some form of artificial intelligence, including computers that replicate themselves, intelligent data bases and corporate expert systems and readers. Among the firms are Artificial Intelligence Corp. from Dartmouth, Cognitive Systems, Inc. from Yale, Teknowledge, Inc. from Stanford and Symbolics, Inc. from MIT.

The heating up of the American effort has come, to some degree, as a response to the well-publicized Japanese Fifth Generation computer project, which was formed specifically to succeed at designing human intelligence into a computer by 1990. This $450 million Japanese government-backed plan represents the greatest challenge to the United States' longstanding superiority in high-technology. Considering the prodigious multilayered American design for artificial-intelligence research, it is clear that the Japanese threat is not being taken lightly.

With all of this movement in the field, researchers are now—after suffering through the disappointments since 1956—once again enthused about the potential for their discipline. Dr. Edward Feigenbaum of Stanford, who recently studied the Japanese Fifth Generation project extensively, compares artificial intelligence to traditional computing in an analogy that contains a heady dose of optimism: "The change from the speed of walking—about four miles an hour—to the speed of automobiles—about forty miles an hour—was an order of magnitude change that . . . has transformed our lives utterly. The next great order of magnitude change, from automobiles to jet planes that travel at four hundred miles an hour, has made equivalent transformations in our lives. This is central to . . . the new generation of [artificially intelligent] computers: quantitative changes in computing speed, power and reason that must make qualitative changes in our lives we can barely foresee. As for the computers that most of us are familiar with right now, they aren't horseless carriages. They're no more than bicycles."

Chapter 4

# ON MINING HEURISTICS AND KNOWLEDGE

Each age has its artifacts, tools indelibly stamped with the mark of the humans who crafted them. The prime artifact of this century is the computer. Perhaps the computer is even the quintessential artifact, because it excels in skills —number and data manipulation—unique, until now, to people. Whatever the case, by attempting to create machines that go well beyond calculating to actually think, artificial-intelligence theorists are raising the technological stakes. Researchers in the discipline are creating artifacts that for the first time not only bear the mark of their creators, but are also made in their makers' image. And as builders of the first artificially intelligent computers that are being used in the real world, those who design expert systems—computers that replicate the cognitive skills of masters in their fields—consider themselves to be civilization's most sophisticated artificers.

"We are basically engineers who are constructing *the* artifacts of the high-tech period," says Edward Feigenbaum, computer science professor at Stanford University and one of the leading voices in California's artificial-intelligence community. On his university's Palo Alto campus and at the start-up corporations in nearby Silicon Valley nearly all of the significant expert-system research and construction in this country is taking place. "The flavor of our enterprise is build and test, measure, rebuild, and retest. There's a strict engineering bias to our work. Like all artificial-intelligence workers we're studying intelligence, but we're primarily interested in seeing it emerge in artifacts."

The creators of expert systems are prototypical applied scientists; their computers are intended for immediate hands-on use. Their machines' validity is judged primarily by how well they function in society, not by how much they will eventually teach us about ourselves and how we think. In that, they offer the first practical look at applied artificial intelligence.

If the artifact is the computer—the expert system itself—then its principal moving part is knowledge. Yet knowledge, to the builders of expert systems, is not understood in the traditional sense. Instead, they have created a unique definition of knowledge, one that assures that their computers will never be confused with the chess-playing computers or the data-bound problem-solving machines that artificial intelligence first embraced.

The early artificial-intelligence programs, such as Newell and Simon's Logic Theory Machine, treated knowledge in Alan Turing's terms. Their designers assumed that knowledge is purely information that could be formalized, codified and then programmed in computer languages. They were convinced that this raw data is the primary component of human thought and intelligence. And at the same time, they gave short shrift to the notion that the strategies people use to manipulate information are essential factors in the intelligence puzzle. These programs were, thus, unidimensional. And the one dimension they contained—massive doses of data—was far less consequential than many of the other properties of intelligence.

The most current research into the mind and computers has totally dismissed the idea that packaging raw data for bulk ingestion by computers—the brute-force programming method—is the key to cognitive modeling. Instead, recent work shows that the more complex and sophisticated pathways to problem solving—such as the heuristics people use to latch onto relevant data and reject the irrelevant—are of paramount importance, indeed, the operand in human intelligence. The builders of expert systems today lean heavily on this line of thinking as they define and structure the knowledge they program into their computers.

"Knowledge in expert systems is a melange of facts, prejudices, beliefs, and, most important, heuristic strategies," says Feigenbaum. "By working with heuristics as our central programming trick we cannot predict that the computer's results will be always useful as absolutely as those working with conventional programming algorithms can. But conventional algorithms offer you nothing more than the chance to build dumb, inflexible data bases. Algorithms will never produce machine intelligence. Programmed heuristics, on the other hand, can make the computer provide results that are at once efficient and intelligent. And these results are specific enough most of the time to be useful." Feigenbaum's statement descends from Ernest Kent's description of heuristics as strategies that "find adequate solutions to complex problems as opposed to exact solutions to simpler ones."

Expert systems presently in use cover a broad range of difficult tasks. One is proficient in diesel-engine repair; another in computer design; and still another in telephone-line troubleshooting. What's more, there are expert systems working in the most critical disciplines, such as medicine and chemical molecular analysis. These last in particular, developed within academia, are yielding essential clues to the efficacy of a huge number of heuristical thought strategies.

By all accounts the quintessential expert system is Mycin, a program developed at Stanford in the mid-1970s, that diagnoses and recommends drug treatments for blood and meningitis infections. Mycin is a computer that contains the combined knowledge—used in the broad sense of the word adopted by today's artificial-intelligence researchers—of Stanford University physicians Drs. Axline, Cohen, Fellows and Yu. The chief designer of Mycin is Edward Shortliffe, assistant professor of medicine and computer science at the university.

Shortliffe is one of a growing number of medical practitioners actively integrating computers into health care. Ironically, while physicians have been, as a group, far slower than other professionals to adopt data processing and office-automation technology, they have been attracted to the value of computers with artificial intelligence as clinical and diagnostic aids. Many doctors are now involved in interdisciplinary research that combines computers with medicine, resulting in such diverse high-tech breakthroughs as teleradiology, nuclear magnetic resonance, ultrasound devices and now, powerful expert systems.

A great deal of ambition and unswerving devotion to the idea of computerizing and modernizing medicine is required to achieve success in mixing the two disciplines, as Shortliffe's schizophrenic and energetic academic career shows. "I discovered computers in college, in the late 1960s at Harvard, and really enjoyed them," Shortliffe says. "Yet I also had for some time been thinking about going into medicine. I was fortunate to be directed to the laboratory of Dr. Octo Barnett and his group at Massachusetts General Hospital in Boston where I went to work as a student research assistant. They were doing some of the early landmark research in using computers in clinical settings. I began to realize there that maybe I didn't need to choose between the two fields."

The primary figure who led him to this conclusion was his mentor at Massachusetts General, Dr. Robert Greenaes, who was at the time completing a PhD in computer science after having received an MD from Harvard. Hearing that Shortliffe wanted to emulate Greenaes's achievement, Dr. Barnett, who is still a leading force in medical computing, advised him to attend Stanford for graduate work, because "it is one of the few medical schools in the United States that has a highly elective curriculum which allows a student to customize his course selection if he has weird interests."

In 1970, Shortliffe began his work at Stanford Medical

School, and he immediately became a constant presence at the university's computer science department, hoping to find some kindred spirits who were also interested in combining health care with computers. There he touched base for the first time with artificial intelligence. He met Edward Feigenbaum, who was already constructing prototypes of the very first expert systems, mostly for chemical and genetic analyses, who spoke to him about how significant a role these computers could play in medicine. Shortliffe was intrigued and bolstered by Feigenbaum's work. His curiosity was not only piqued, it was jolted to the point where he convinced the school to allow him to design his own PhD program.

"I created a six-year MD/PhD," Shortliffe says, "in medical information sciences, essentially a combination of computer sciences and medicine. During the first two years of medical school, I took both medical courses and computer science courses. Then my third and fourth years were devoted to full-time research in which I began to create a plan for how artificial intelligence might be used in medicine. These were the first years of the Mycin project development. Then in my fifth and sixth years I had to go back and be a medical student on the wards. But fortunately I was able to maintain enough involvement with the medical-computing community that it was not too hard to get back into work with Mycin when I finished my clinical training."

Shortliffe was one of the first researchers in the country to successfully program knowledge based on subjective judgments and rules of thumb into a computer. He pried into the clinical expertise of Drs. Axline, Cohen, Fellows, and Yu, hoping to create a series of blueprints that show

how, piece by piece, they construct a diagnosis and treatment plan for patients with blood and meningitis infections. "We tried to capsulize the specific steps that our experts took in the treatment of individual patients," Shortliffe says, "into general rules that can stand on their own as overall statements of fact or inferential knowledge to be used when treating *all* patients. Often these rules were very much based on the expert's experiences rather than on any statistical analysis he may have done on a lot of data. Someone who has been in practice for a number of years gets a certain sense of what combinations of factors might mean in a given case, and this is what characterizes expertise."

Out of the discussions with the four experts, over two hundred rules or medical heuristics were divined and programmed into the computer. The heuristics were written in the form of a premise (*if*) and a conclusion (*then*). The following rule, for instance, is used by the computer to identify an organism infecting the patient:

Rule 037

IF 1) the stain of the organism is gramneg (the organism is unable to hold an injected purple dye), and
2) the morphology of the organism is rod, and
3) the aerobicity of the organism is facultative (the organism is able to thrive under many sets of conditions),

THEN there is strongly suggestive evidence (.8)

that the class of the organism is enterobacteriaceae.

If the premise conditions are true, then the conclusion can be accepted as factual knowledge, at least to a quantitative degree of certainty. In the terms of Rule 037, if the bacterial organism is a facultative aerobe and it is a gram negative rod, then there is an 80 percent (.8) certainty that it can be identified as of the enterobacteriaceae.

This simple statement is a common rule of thumb physicians use when working with infectious blood and spinal diseases. It is one of the heuristic-based pathways they unconsciously turn to to build treatment plans for their patients. Programmed into a computer, the statement becomes a powerful tool, a carefully designed catalyst of machine intelligence. Like a human expert, the computer, armed with two hundred heuristics similar to Rule 037, now knows how to diagnose many infectious blood and spinal diseases.

But without specific information about a given patient's condition, the computer is, of course, unable to offer any advice at all. It is the doctor who must consult blood tests and use direct examinations to gather data about patients; the computer must rely on a physician to provide this information. Thus, the computer must engage in a dialogue with its consulting doctor; using the information it receives from the physician it works toward a diagnosis and provides treatment advice.

Here is an example of the dialoging process:

Mycin: I will refer to the most recent positive culture for which you desire therapeutic advice as

Culture-1

From what site was the specimen for Culture-1 taken?
MD: Blood
Mycin: I will refer to the first offending organism from this blood culture (Culture-1) as

Organism-1

Enter the identity (genus) of Organism-1:
MD: Unknown
Mycin: Staining characteristics of Organism-1:
MD: Gramneg
Mycin: Is Organism-1 a rod or coccus (etc.)?
MD: Rod
Mycin: What is the aerobicity of Organism-1:
MD: Facultative

Mycin operates by what is called "backchaining through a problem." It first attempts to identify which information it or its human counterpart positively knows. In this case, it asks: Do I know or can I find out from the consulting MD what Organism-1 is? If the answer is negative, as it was above, Mycin then asks a variety of questions to reach a positive conclusion.

As illustrated in the example, the computer is attempting to identify the bacteria that has infected the patient. When the doctor says that he does not know the name of the organism's species, Mycin, aware that it can be any variety of species from pseudomonas to enterobacteriaceae, proceeds to ascertain which one it is—taking each possibility separately—by asking a series of test questions (questions culled from the "If" portion of its rules). If any line of questioning is inconclusive, Mycin holds it in abeyance and moves on to probe the physician with questions relating to other species the bacteria might be.

For example, had the MD not been able to tell Mycin anything about the aerobicity of the bacteria while he was still certain about its coloring and shape, the computer would have been forced to ignore enterobacteriaceae as a conclusion for the time being and it would have moved on to ask questions about the next most likely bacteria species. A new line of inquiry would be initiated:

Mycin: Is the patient a burn patient?

[The thrust of this question is unorthodox. The MD, confused by it, might decide to examine Mycin's motives.]

MD: Why?

[In response, Mycin regurgitates the analysis it is pursuing.]

Mycin: This will aid in determining the class of Organism-1. It has already been established (from the physician's previous answers) that
  1) the morphology of Organism-1 is rod, and
  2) the stain of Organism-1 is gramneg.
Therefore, IF
  3) the patient has been seriously burned
THEN
  there is weakly suggestive evidence (.4) that the identity of the organism is pseudomonas.

Backchaining, in order to move from a hypothesis to a conclusion, and the method Mycin uses to separate what it can implicitly accept as fact from what it still needs to find out to reach a firm conclusion, are heuristic strategies used frequently by people. Mycin's well-chosen questions show that if a goal is first well defined—in this case, to identify a species of bacteria from among perhaps ten possibilities—steps can be taken to achieve it.

Recall the example in Chapter 2 of how people use both of Mycin's heuristic methods. The man who was offered $1 million if he reached Atlantic City had his goal clearly in mind. He simply had to backchain from this goal to make sure he had all the answers necessary to reach it. First he separated what he knew about how to get to Atlantic City from what he needed to know. Then he backchained through the questions in his "need to know" list to arrive at useful answers.

Mycin does not work at the torrid pace of this would-be Atlantic City traveler. While our traveler can create a detailed and correct plan of action in perhaps ten or fifteen minutes, the computer's dialogue with its consulting doctor usually continues for about 45 questions (and almost two hours) before the expert system is able to reach a diagnosis and offer a treatment plan.

---

Mycin: My therapy recommendation will be based on the following possible identities of the organism(s) that seem to be significant:

Item 1: The identity of Organism-1 may be pseudomonas

Item 2: The identity of Organism-1 may be klebsiella

Item 3: The identity of Organism-1 may be enterobacteriaceae

Item 4: The identity of Organism-1 may be e. coli

Item 5: The identity of Organism-1 may be proteus (species unknown)

Does Patient-1 have a clinically significant allergic reaction to any antimicrobial agent?

MD: No

Mycin: My preferred therapy recommendation is as follows:

In order to cover for Items 1,2,3,4,5;

Give the following in combination:
1) Gentamicin
   Dose: 1.7 mg/kg q8h—im
   Comments: Modify dose in renal failure
2) Carbenicillin
   Dose: 25 mg/kg q2h—iv
   Comments: Modify dose in renal failure

Mycin is impressive, even when it is tested against human capabilities. When it was submitted to a group of experts on meningitis and infectious blood diseases for evaluation, in 90 percent of the cases a majority of the judges said that the program's decisions were the same as or better than the decisions they would have made.

Still, because of some severe shortcomings, Mycin has never been used in a full-fledged clinical setting. Its principal failing is its lack of medical worldliness, a failing that could be described as its chronic Achilles' heel. "As we got to know Mycin well, we realized that there was a huge amount that the system simply did not know," says Shortliffe. "Mycin knew about blood bacterias and meningitis bacterias, but it was hardly an infectious disease expert. It knew nothing about pneumonia, urinary tract infections, brain abscesses and many other important infectious diseases. It would be risky to use it as a consultation system, and to tell hospitals, 'Here's an infectious disease consultation system, but use it only in cases of bacteremia or meningitis.' To this day people are experimenting with the system and trying to run cases of venereal disease through it. Of course, it always fails." Mycin is also an extremely slow system. The fact that it can take as long as two hours to consult on a case makes most physicians who have used it impatient.

Its implicit value, though, resides in its being one of the first computers to show how a machine can capture and use sophisticated clinical expertise to reach its own decisions. And recognition of this has resulted in a rash of expert systems modeled on Mycin. One of the more noteworthy of these is Puff, a computer that is used to interpret pulmonary-function test results for the Pacific Medical Center in San Francisco.

Puff has earned a great deal of approbation as a practical computer colleague with at least a limited degree of intelligence. Examined closely, though, its success is based on the fact that it, too, is fluent in only a very restricted domain. Puff is made up of fifty heuristic strategies—one-fourth of Mycin's knowledge base—and it is strictly an examiner of test results. Lung volumes, blood counts, oxygen respiration levels and the like represent the full extent of the data that Puff will ever see or know about.

Some artificial-intelligence researchers, however, most of whom willingly credit Mycin and its progeny with being the first true purveyors of human cognitive processes on a computer, believe that this line of artifact building will never lead to the replication of intelligence on a broader level and in the most complex situations.

"Mycin shows that the big diagnostic problems, those that cover multiple-simultaneous diseases, for instance, are impossible to squeeze into if/then rules. It's very hard for a physician to express his heuristical strategies to fit in the formal, airtight compartments that Mycin demands." So says James A. Reggia, a neurologist at the University of Maryland Hospital in Baltimore. Dr. Reggia, who has spent ten years closely examining expert systems in general and medical diagnosis expert systems in particular, rejects the so-called rule-based computers as too inflexible and too rigid to truly emulate the way physicians—and people in general—think. "One of the biggest problems with rule-based systems is that all of the possible contexts for a rule's application must be included in its antecedent [if] clauses," says Reggia. "Since all of the relevant factors for applying a rule are not always obvious or of a high enough degree of possibility, this can result in errors of omission in the antecedents of rules."

What Reggia is saying is illustrated best by examining the following hypothetical rule:

> IF cumulonimbus clouds are present, and the humidity is 75 percent or higher, and the sky is a dark gray,
> THEN there is a strong certainty (.8) that it will rain within one hour.

Of course, while this rule is useful and accurate most of the time, there is an error of omission that is not immediately obvious but could be critical if this computer is to predict the weather as an expert would. The omission is simply that even if all of the antecedents are found to be correct, a solar eclipse—and not a rain storm—may be ensuing. A human weather expert would know—and be able to retrieve this fact from an almost-forgotten recess of his mind—that an eclipse is an uncommon but not impossible occurrence. The computer, on the other hand, tied inexorably to its set of rules related to its limited domain, cannot fathom such an event.

If the possibility of an eclipse is programmed into the expert system, however, its complex of rules would become necessarily unwieldly—and slow. Understanding a solar eclipse requires access to a sophisticated series of facts ranging from the moon's moment-by-moment location to its revolutionary path. For the infinitesimal probability that a solar eclipse is indeeed occurring, it is a waste of computer memory space and programmer time to consider creating rules around it. Thus, it is the more temporal, subtle and unexpected events of life that the rule-based expert system is unable to comprehend.

Reggia describes a similar situation where a medical expert system would fall short: "The meaning of a unilateral dilated and fixed pupil depends on whether long-tract findings are present, whether a patient is awake or unconscious, whether the neck is subtle or rigid and so forth. If one attempts to incorporate all of this relevant context into antecedent clauses there can be a very rapid growth in the number of rules present."

Reggia's analysis of how rule-based expert systems fall short led him to disavow them. And building his own theory of expert systems, one that would permit more worldly computers, has become his central professional goal. His obsession has been time consuming, and has made for a schizophrenic career. While he remains a practicing neurologist, he now crams the work of a computer scientist and artificial-intelligence researcher into his limited hours away from medicine.

Reggia first became interested in expert systems as a young physician in the early 1970s when the stories of Mycin began to circulate throughout the health-care community. Even then, he felt intuitively that as they were being constructed, expert systems would have severe limitations. To find out if this were true or not, he returned to school to get a PhD in computer science.

Since that time he has become more convinced than ever that his hunches about Mycin were correct. He studied physicians to determine how they reach diagnoses and create treatment plans for patients. He investigated the few analyses conducted by others of how physicians make decisions. Reggia was hoping to find precise models of diagnostic reasoning—different from those used in Mycin—that he could pattern his expert systems after. He was patently successful, and what has emerged from his work, though still in the early testing stage, is a possible breakthrough in artificial-intelligence research that could enlarge the grasp of expert systems significantly.

Reggia found that physicians—and people generally, he feels—reach conclusions after juggling interim hypotheses and probing their validity long enough to prove one or more of them correct. Reggia calls this a hypothesize-and-test process. It has ties to backchaining—as in Mycin—but unlike Mycin, this theory assumes that humans think in a parallel fashion by considering a group of possible conclusions at once, and not in a serial, strictly piece-by-piece fashion. In essence, we simultaneously analyze competing solutions for each given situation we face. When one solution so dominates that it is deemed to be correct, we then take action using it as a guidepost.

"Looking at it the way physicians operate," Reggia says, "during the hypothesize-and-test process, they construct a 'model' of the patient. This model is based on what symptoms are known to be present. It postulates the presence of one or more elementary hypotheses, diseases in this case, that could explain the patient's manifestations. In general, the hypothesis structure consists of competing explanations for the patient's problems. The model of the patient being constructed will likely presume the simultaneous presence of multiple diseases." The physician then proceeds to test each hypothesis for validity and arrives at a diagnosis that is flexible and open to be changed as the symptoms do.

Decision making, as Reggia describes it, is bilayered. The outer layer contains the many hypotheses simultaneously under consideration, each waiting to be discarded or accepted. The inner layer contains the questions and uncertainties surrounding each of the separate hypotheses. As Reggia sees it, rule-based expert systems simply cannot contend with this labyrinth of partial and possible conclusions.

To create a system that would work, Reggia set out to design an artificial-intelligence program that could examine an individual hypothesis in fuller ways than Mycin. In essence, he took groups of closely related Mycin-like rules and condensed them into what he calls *frames*. These frames are intended to be made up of around twenty if/then rules, thereby turning a series of complicated rules into one self-contained unit. He joined with two colleagues at the University of Maryland computer department, Drs. Dana Nau and Pearl Y. Wang, to create this more adequate, and more humanlike, computer.

They began by looking at basilar migraines. A doctor's description of this condition would be: "Basilar migraine usually occurs in a young adult between twenty and thirty years of age although it may occur up to fifty years of age. Basilar migraine causes dizziness which is usually vertiginous in nature and either episodic (typically lasting hours) or acute and persistent. It causes headache, most often in an occipital location."

"How would you encode basilar migraine in an if/then rule system?" Reggia asks. "Perhaps:

IF age <= 50 and dizziness, headache, etc.,
are present,
THEN conclude basilar migraine.

But that is clearly insufficient. It does not account for the fact that basilar migraine is more common between the ages of twenty and thirty, that there are certain types of dizziness present of various durations and so on. To program this information into if/then rules would require an incredibly large number of rules, interacting in increasingly complicated ways."

Reggia, Nau and Wang succeeded in tieing the entire

description of basilar migraine into one frame that elegantly winds like a spiral staircase among the more subtle aspects of the diagnosis. A portion of the frame looks like this (A = always; H = high likelihood; L = low likelihood; N = never):

```
BASILAR MIGRAINE
  DESCRIPTION
    AGE =
      20 THRU 30   (H);
      30 THRU 50   (L);
      50 THRU 110  (N);
    DIZZINESS =
      TYPE—VERTIGO (H);
           REST    (L);
      COURSE—EPISODIC
                  EPISODE DURATION—MINUTES (L);
                                   HOURS   (H);
                                   DAYS    (L);
                ACUTE AND PERSISTENT (A);
    HEAD PAIN =
      LOCATION—OCCIPITAL (H);
               REST      (L);
```

Reggia feels that a computer embedded with two hundred such frames, each describing a separate diagnosis of an illness, could overcome Mycin's chief problem of not being a complete medical expert.

"Given one or more initial symptoms," Reggia says, "a medical diagnosis system of this type could pull out the frames carrying the hypotheses that potentially would explain those symptoms. Those chosen hypotheses are then tested in the sense that they are measured for their ability to account for the known facts about the patient. The system generates questions to help it discriminate among the most likely hypotheses, and then recycles through this entire process again as it picks up additional information from its questioning." Reggia stresses that the questions his computer asks may go beyond verbal ones, and include physical examinations of the patient or the ordering of laboratory tests.

Reggia's frame-based expert systems offer great promise and could soon replace traditional expert systems. By all accounts, they come much closer to human associative and inferential processes than their predecessors. However, while his diagnosis frames are holding up well under testing and offer efficiency that if/then rules never could, the outer layer of decision making, where a number of hypotheses are simultaneously juggled, is a sticking point in the research. Computer memory is pushed over its limit by the voluminous data involved in considering groups of hypotheses at once. Reggia is working on developing a system that maintains an entirely separate and concurrent data base to hold the outer layer, while the inner layer—where frames reside—is being tested for validity. If this works Reggia will have created a computer that has the ability to manipulate separate layers of thought at the same time, a trait that up to now only people possess.

"I know we're on the right path," Reggia says. "But I

can't claim ascendancy over traditional Mycin-like expert systems, because they have proven, though limited, results and my designs only have a more efficacious theory to offer. It will still be a few years before a judgment can be made."

Whatever the judgment is and no matter how well-rounded a medical expert Reggia's program becomes, it will never be able to leave the domain of making decisions about diagnoses and treatments. In that, it is a jack of one trade. Some in artificial intelligence see this as a problem that must be reckoned with. They feel that for a computer to be called intelligent—as one would use that term when describing a person—it has to be the master of a variety of subjects, not just one.

Most artificial-intelligence researchers have avoided tackling this central shortcoming of expert systems. It seems like an issue with too many theoretical trapdoors. But one researcher, Jaime Carbonell, a computer science professor at Carnegie-Mellon University in Pittsburgh, feels that it is a research dilemma that must be confronted at any cost. The ability to create machines that possess intelligence in two or more domains, he says, is vital to the future of artificial intelligence as a discipline. For artificial intelligence to prosper scientifically, he feels, a nonprovincial computer, in human terms, must be designed.

Carbonell says that the main failing of expert systems is that their designers have left a key element of human intelligence out of the programs—the ability to use situation-to-situation analogies. They have thus eliminated any chance for these systems to learn from previous experience and in the process doomed expert systems to one-domain capabilities. According to Carbonell, people turn to analogies as a way to transfer previously learned knowledge to new, seemingly unrelated situations. Analogies, Carbonell says, are some of our most frequently used heuristic strategies.

"Consider a person who knows how to drive a car and is asked to drive a truck," says Carbonell. "Such a person may have no general plan or procedure for driving trucks, but is likely to perform most of the steps correctly by transferring much of his or her automobile driving knowledge. Would that we had expert systems and robots that were so self-adaptable to new tasks."

Sharing quarters with the computer science department, Jaime Carbonell and the other CMU artificial-intelligence researchers are housed in a long and sprawling structure that extends along one side of a grassy rectangular area. Affectionately known as the "elephant building," it dwarfs all the other facilities nestled among the gently rolling hills of the campus.

From inside the elephant building, the haunt of the artificial-intelligence researchers appears somewhat less inspiring. The atmosphere is stark and serious. Each of the academics is crowded into a tiny cubicle or a moderately sized office, sometimes two to a cubbyhole. Adding to the spartan interior fare are ubiquitous gray cinder-block walls and the murky yellow-green rug.

Carbonell's small office is a reflection of the dedicated workaholic he is. His desk is piled high with books, pamphlets and papers; the desk blotter is liberally sprinkled with the graffiti of artificial intelligence—formulas and calculations; there are tables covered with uneven stacks of journals, printouts and loose papers, all tattered from what could be called academic ingestion; and his bookshelves, which relieve the monotony of the cinder-block wall design, are crowded. If there is a pattern to all this, it is impossible to decipher.

There is, however, a pattern to Carbonell's research message. He constantly and continually chides expert-system designers for not understanding how important analogies are to the way people learn. He sees it as a severe blind spot in artificial intelligence. To Carbonell, creators of expert systems are guilty of taking a remarkable technology and completely inhibiting it when it needn't be handcuffed.

"We have to ask the question," Carbonell says in explaining how analogies are used as learning tools, " 'What makes a new problem that people are facing somehow familiar and solvable?' Clearly a major aspect consists of the person being reminded of past situations that bear strong similarity to the present problem. This type of reminding experience serves to retrieve behaviors that were appropriate in earlier problem-solving episodes. Past behavior is adapted to meet the demands of the current situation.

"We should concentrate on reproducing this process on a computer. The analogy is a way that the computer, embedded with rules based on heuristics, can learn by looking for correspondences among its data. This means that the computer will be able to notice similarities across multiple situations."

Carbonell describes an utterly unscientific, informal experiment he conducted on five history and art students that nonetheless convinced him of the importance of analogical learning to people. "I told the students to prove that the product of two even numbers is even," says Carbonell. "None of the five was able to solve this simple algebraic problem although all five made serious attempts. Continuing with the experiment, I explained how to arrive at the proof carefully enough to ensure that all five subjects understood it."

After Carbonell detailed how the proof is reached, all five students claimed to understand his explanation and expressed dismay for not having figured it out themselves. Then Carbonell asked them to prove that the product of two odd numbers is odd. "I could feel the grim determination to succeed this time among the students," Carbonell says. "Three of them succeeded. But what was more important is that this informal experiment indicated clearly that the second problem was solved by analogy from the solution to the first problem. The scratch papers collected from the students suggested direct attempts at transferring and modifying steps of the first solution."

As to transferring the analogy theory onto a computer and teaching computers to learn by this method, Carbonell's first breakthrough came recently in the field of geometry. It is instructive to note that many artificial-intelligence researchers find that their initial efforts are involved with reasoning and logic using mathematical problems. This is simply because math presents very formal and constrained information and heuristic paths with which to work. It is, without question, one of the most structured domains that exist and, thus, closest to the computer's temperament.

"We first tried to do very simple geometry problems," Carbonell says, "like having the computer prove two line segments congruent and then asking the computer to take this proof and by analogy transfer it to proving two angles congruent." He programmed into the machine enough pure data about geometry and the heuristics used for geometrical proofs for the computer to think intelligently about lines, angles, the formation of shapes and the like.

"In terms of the analogy," Carbonell continues, "the first thing that has to happen is that the machine has to recognize from what it knows already that the second problem of congruent angles is similar to the first problem of congruent lines." In other words, rather than merely thinking in terms of one problem—i.e., how can it be proved that two lines are congruent—and then forgetting it until the next time the same question is asked, the computer, in this case, retains and understands the concept of congruency. It is then able to apply the concept to all related questions.

One of the human heuristic strategies the computer is taught is called memory indexing, or tagging. This heuristic is borrowed from neuroscientists who view the brain as an organic library. People, it seems, store information with identifier tags like library catalog index cards, so that we can access specific data as needed without reading the entire library.

Neurobiologist Gary Lynch, of the University of California at Irvine, described this procedure: "We appear to file information in much the same way books are stored on a library shelf. We have a row of memories related to the subject, and that row will itself be in a section related to the subject, and that section will be in the part of the library where we stored memories of similar informational contexts. Then when we go back to retrieve a memory, we seem to go back down through the hierarchy."

In the same fashion, Carbonell instructs his computer to tag information that is broader than facts, information that could be called conceptual or general—such as congruency—and thus potentially useful by analogy to solve a variety of specific problems. "The program is designed to then search its knowledge base very selectively by wading through its indexed data [its tags] first in hopes of finding a past problem that has an agreed-upon number of similarities to the present problem," Carbonell says. "In this case it hits upon congruency as the overall conceptually related problem. This is because while we're dealing with angles instead of line segments, there are many aspects of congruency that are the same, like the number of angles equals the number of line segments and so on. Then it attempts a transformation process between the old problem and the new one." What is especially remarkable about Carbonell's approach is that during this transformation process the computer literally teaches itself new knowledge based on what it knows already.

Carbonell is encouraged by his success in imparting theories of geometry to a computer, and he continues to perfect this aspect of artificial intelligence. Yet at the same time, he is tackling something far more ambitious that, because of the complex nature of the domains involved, will probably not prove out for a much longer time.

In a new research effort called the Fermi Project, Carbonell has returned to the subject he majored in as an undergraduate, physics. He is currently teaching a computer to become an expert in this field. Then, through the use of analogical reasoning, he will attempt to induce the computer to teach itself some of the rudiments of chemistry. "There are enough similarities between the two fields for me to be encouraged that this will work," Carbonell says. But not immediately, he adds. "Most of the larger expert-system projects have turned out to require that a dozen or more people work full-time for three to five years. This is because they are so knowledge-intensive. It takes a huge amount of knowledge to be programmed into the system first before the system itself will perform smartly."

Carbonell's research is on a path that many in artificial intelligence see as sure to prove out and carry expert systems to appreciably more significant heights than much of the other research in this field. However, despite his lofty perch in the realm of expert-system design, Carbonell, in the statement above, makes it clear that he shares the same frustrations as his colleagues. All expert-system developers, whether they are using an approach similar to Mycin's, Reggia's, or Carbonell's, have been heard to utter the same plaint: Programming knowledge—i.e., identifying human heuristics and turning them into computer rules—is a tedious and imposing task that takes too many years to accomplish well. And what makes this task seem even more intractable is that the researchers are not usually the ones responsible for cataloging the program's necessary heuristics. The job of prying cognitive rules of thumb out of experts goes, instead, to people known as knowledge engineers.

Because knowledge and heuristics are the most important components in an expert system, knowledge engineering takes on a critical importance in the design of an expert system. Knowledge engineering done poorly can destroy even the best-planned expert system; done well, it can raise the value of a mediocre one measurably. "It may sound overly obvious but it must never be forgotten," Edward Feigenbaum of Stanford says, "that an expert system performs well to the extent that it is knowledgeable about its area of expertise and it performs poorly to the extent that it is ill-informed about its domain."

There are only a few hundred knowledge engineers nationwide—and perhaps fifty good ones—so the craft retains a mysterious aura in artificial-intelligence circles. They are deemed by some to be a hybrid of alchemist and translator. They—and they alone—carry knowledge in its most meaningful form between the human being and the computer.

"Knowledge engineering is expensive, it's time consuming, it's boring," says Stephen J. Andriole, a former Defense Department high-technology contracts administrator and now a designer of expert systems that are to advise military chiefs in the field during wartime. Because Andriole has a strong academic background in computers, he is one of the few expert-systems designers who does his own knowledge engineering. "The less patient artificial-intelligence designers too often want to start building rules into their systems immediately. Well, you can't do that. Knowledge engineering may seem like a long process that shows no results for a good while. But you've got to spend a lot of time actually identifying and defining the knowledge that you'd like to incarnate into the computer program."

Because of their indispensable role in creating expert systems, and because the demand for their services is increasingly outstripping supply, knowledge engineers are, more and more, becoming something of a nuisance to artificial-intelligence researchers. With so few capable knowledge engineers and so many more needed literally each academic term, a builder of expert systems is often forced to slow down his timetable while he waits for the knowledge acquisition to be completed. Feigenbaum describes this succinctly: "Knowledge engineering constitutes the single biggest bottleneck in the progress toward efficient artifact building. It stands in the way of getting it done fast and inexpensively. It's ironic that the knowledge engineer, who's really responsible, in the end for the success of the expert system, is also the chief bottleneck in the process." Feigenbaum's insight cannot easily be faulted. He is quite familiar with the critical nature of knowledge engineering, since he was the first person ever to work as a knowledge engineer, when he was involved in building the earliest expert systems during the 1960s.

Edward Feigenbaum is a peppery man who is known for regaling visitors about the virtues and importance of artificial intelligence and how the discipline fits into the full scheme of humanity's evolution. Perhaps better than anyone else working in the artificial-intelligence field, he knows the power of its potential, having experienced firsthand the wrongheadedness of the 1950s and then the emergence of the far more productive heuristical programming during the next decade. His career, in fact, has been a whirlwind tour through the scientific premises bracing artificial intelligence, a coming of age that has now firmly implanted this New Jersey-born scientist as the chief spokesman for the West Coast expert-systems builders.

Feigenbaum first heard about artificial intelligence in 1956 when he was an undergraduate studying under Herbert Simon in the business school at Carnegie-Tech University. That was the year, of course, that Simon had enraptured the artificial-intelligence community at the Dartmouth conference with the severely flawed Logic Theory Machine he created along with Alan Newell. The Carnegie-Tech professor, upon returning from Dartmouth, told his students, in hyperbolic and glowing terms, about the New Hampshire conclave and the reception he had received there. Feigenbaum, whose interest in business was essentially fueled by wanting to learn about problem solving, was taken by Simon's work and how it meshed—on a philosophical level, at least—with investigating and understanding the way people arrive at answers to complex questions.

Feigenbaum drank in Simon's concepts until he had a chance to do his own work in the primitive field of artificial intelligence about two years later, when he attended graduate school at the University of California at Berkeley. Concurrently, he received a $70,000 grant from the Carnegie Corporation of New York to study the computer modeling of human information processing, learning and decision making. Seventy thousand dollars was an incredibly inflated amount for that period, and especially for such a young academic. At the time, even fully tenured professors rarely saw so much as a $10,000 grant during their entire careers. But the high figure reflected the increased premium being placed on artificial-intelligence research, the one enduring and valuable result of the Dartmouth conference.

Feigenbaum's work during the life of this grant, while lacking in tangible achievements, produced one noteworthy outcome: It convinced those who followed his research that only intensive examinations into human behavior could lead to artificial intelligence. The elementary information he gained about the way people solve problems and the theoretical insight into heuristics he derived from the neuroscientists and cognitive researchers who assisted him during this period served him in good stead when he moved to Stanford in 1965, this time to the computer department, and began to build the first expert systems.

At the Palo Alto campus, while he was building the expert system known as Dendral, Feigenbaum performed the first full-scale piece of knowledge engineering. To build Dendral he probed the minds of expert chemists and programmed into the computer the heuristics they use for determining the exact structure of individual chemicals found in larger compound molecules.

Feigenbaum's work as a knowledge engineer set the standard for much of the knowledge engineering that has ensued. Knowledge engineering, as Feigenbaum defined it, is a rigorous craft that requires enormous self-discipline and an uncanny amount of perception to be successful. Despite sounding like a flippant ad slogan for a computer firm, it is a formal, systematic method of pursuing knowledge.

First, of course, it requires the expert's full participation. "Typically that can be a very difficult aspect of the whole operation—to convince an expert to devote the considerable time it takes to examine his thought processes," Feigenbaum says. "But while experts are quite busy, for a variety of reasons—not the least of which is the prospect of being immortalized in a machine—they can frequently be persuaded to cooperate. At that point the project can begin with the knowledge engineer drowning himself in information about the field through textbooks, articles and abstracts. In part he is trying to learn more about the expert and in part he is trying to alert himself to the jargon and issues that are important to those in the particular domain being studied."

Following this, the knowledge engineer is ready for the first interview with the expert. A steady evolution has occurred in the types of interview and recording techniques used during the sessions. Most of the early engineers simply took notes during the one-on-one fact-finding sessions; some used audio tape. Today the more innovative workers in the field are turning to videotape to ensure that their visual observations about the expert and his work are sound. Moreover, many knowledge engineers have stopped using the traditional interview completely, in which an expert is simply asked to describe how he solves problems. They have replaced it with more interesting and thought-provoking decision-making contexts.

"Whatever method is used," Feigenbaum says, "it is important that the expert is posed with fairly difficult problems. First, easy problems show you very little about expertise and secondly, they bore experts to tears. On the other hand, of course, problems have to be simple enough that they do not take days to solve, just hours. This is because if it is a massive problem, it's probably too large to be programmed into a common expert system."

Stephen J. Andriole, in developing his defensive land-military expert system, has elicited heuristics from a group of Defense Department planners at the Army War College in Carlisle, Pennsylvania. His methods exemplify the most advanced knowledge-engineering techniques being used to date. What is strikingly clear from watching him in action is that he does not merely interview his subjects. Instead, he retrieves knowledge by creating situations which replicate the experts' normal working environments.

A diminutive war room serves as headquarters for Andriole's most recent knowledge engineering. There are no huge boards with flashing lights and no computers and printers seemingly in a state of panic as they tick like time bombs à la *Dr. Strangelove* or *War Games*. Instead, maps of various regions of the world line the walls, each of them dotted with red markers for Soviet forces and blue markers delineating the presence of opposing Allied troops. The experts sit around a long conference table, preparing to discuss in a cogent fashion how to fend off an attack from the enemy camp.

Andriole is standing by a map of East and West Germany. Pointing to the East German border and its swath of red, he says: "For the past seventy-two hours, Red has been massing its forces around East Germany. Intelligence suggests that an attack by the Soviets is imminent across the border into West Germany. Intelligence asserts that we have seventy-two hours to deploy Blue forces in such a way as to thwart that attack and repel it. What do we do?"

"I mass half of my forces on the East German border," one Defense Department planner answers as he moves to the map and shifts one-half of the blue markers eastward to lean them up against the red ones.

"Why?"

"Because most likely Red will attack here where they have the greatest strength in numbers."

"But why only half of your forces on the East German border?"

"Because I want to keep the other half in the interior region of the country in case they attempt a twofold incursion. They may use air forces to attack the western part of the country. So I would use the other half of my forces to bolster my own air defense in the different areas of the country away from the eastern border that my intelligence says Red is most interested in."

"What processes did you use in your mind to arrive at your conclusions?" Andriole asks.

The defense experts begin a discussion among themselves to answer this question. They examine their thought processes, seeking to explain how their minds work as they are planning strategic courses of action in the field. After perhaps a half hour, one tells Andriole: "I made a list of the possible courses of action open to the enemy by analyzing its available weaponry, equipment and troops. I then prioritized these courses of action, ranking them in terms of likelihood. And finally I deployed my forces based on my rankings."

Though this is only the first leg of a long journey into the heuristics of his expert DOD planners, Andriole has already learned a great deal about their modes of thinking. Hypothetical strategic defensive maneuvering throughout the world is presented and analyzed for over five hours in this session. Andriole sizes up the constants in their thought processes and, based on these, begins to write sketchy, first-pass, if/then rules to be put into his expert system. He also starts quantifying the rules and the data embedded in them so as to be able to score some more likely to be applicable and to deem others unlikely anomalies.

"It may appear to be overly general at this point," Andriole says, "but these planners have already told me a great many things at this initial session. I know that they are actively estimating the adversary's intentions first; that they are considering the various options and alternatives open to Red and ranking them; and that they are doing a utility assessment from the perspective of the enemy commander in terms of which is the best way to come in, with tanks or land missiles or the like. Finally, to simplify all the data they are attempting to order in their minds, they produce a score sheet that separates the most likely enemy attack plan from the least likely. All of this, in much more detail as I probe deeper and deeper into the experts' ways of thinking, can be captured in the rules of an expert system."

And all of this, significantly, is captured on videotape. Andriole is thus able to view the sessions again and again, to determine any nuances of thought he may have missed by being so closely involved during the decision-making sessions themselves.

The interviews are the first step. They are followed by the building of a template, a framework of rules that provides the first indication of what the programs for the expert system are to look like. And if past experience is any guide, all knowledge engineers agree that when the experts get to look at the template, they will reject it out of hand. They will deny having proposed such a ridiculous set of heuristics; they will categorically reject this design for an expert system as light years away from anything that is useful; this template for an expert system, they will stress, would produce nothing but erroneous advice. Just as we are all our own worst critics when looking into the mirror, the experts are their own worst critics when examining their thought processes.

The experts will be asked to defend the changes in the system they wish to make and the sessions will continue for months on end until something acceptable is created. "The whole process is so stretched out that our best hopes are to have a prototype expert system after eighteen months up and running on computers," Andriole says. "It will be a first cut, very crude, that just approximates really what tactical planning is all about. Hopefully by five to seven years after that we will have an expert computerized tactical planner in the field."

Andriole describes his expert system as "an aggressive one." It will be a checklist for decision making during wartime situations, but what will make it aggressive is that it is designed to actively challenge the Defense Department planners. The planners at the battle site will be able to view a graphic depiction of the strategic situation at hand by looking at the computer screen. The computer will access maps of the region from an attached video disk, and through the same means change the information on its screen as troops and equipment are mobilized in different directions. The planners will then input their plans of action, and the expert system will compare the planners' choices with its own, arrived at by sorting through the heuristic rules and data in its knowledge base. "If the planners' choices and the computer's choices differ," Andriole says, "the computer will respond with, 'That's a dumb idea, why are you doing that? From what I know you really ought to be considering the following moves . . .' "

It is clear from the long hours Andriole is spending on just the knowledge engineering required for his expert system that this process would try the patience of most expert-system developers, who are completely divorced from the knowledge-engineering role itself. This is why, when Edward Feigenbaum first described knowledge engineering as "a bottleneck and hindrance" to artificial intelligence, his statement was greeted with sighs of relief from many expert-system designers. That one so supportive of knowledge engineering could be so critical of it meant that perhaps an approach that would streamline the knowledge-engineering process was in the works. And so it was. Soon after he made his statement, Feigenbaum started taking steps to obliterate the bottleneck knowledge engineering imposes.

Bringing his considerable influence to bear, Feigenbaum and a research group at Stanford University are turning to what they know best—computers—to overcome the impediments of knowledge engineering. They are attempting to automate the process and, in effect, put knowledge engineers out of work. If they succeed, few artificial-intelligence researchers will complain about the sudden onset of unemployment among this group.

Using his already proven expert system Dendral as a guide, Feigenbaum is dissecting its rules in an attempt to discern the nature of heuristic statements and come to some general conclusions as to how they are built. Essentially, he is building an expert system in which the expert being replicated is the knowledge engineer.

Dendral is a complex and esoteric chemical expert system developed in the mid-1960s to take on a task exceedingly crucial to the performance of chemists: something known by the cumbersome term *structure elucidation*. Basically, structure elucidation is similar to doing a crossword puzzle backwards; i.e., writing the across and down clues after you have been given an already filled-in matrix. It is the process of examining a molecular compound made up of unknown elements and then divining those individual elements. This information is used to assay the bonding properties and possible uses of the overall compound in, for instance, pharmacology or toxicology.

The most common device used to determine the chemical structure of a molecule is called a mass spectrometer. This instrument essentially unmasks the compound, breaks it down, analyzes it and then represents it in patterns on a graph. The physical appearance of this graph, which actually shows the way a molecule "fragments" under mass spectroscopy, tells chemists a great deal about the elements buried within the molecule and offers substantial clues as to which substructures they are encountering. But each graph must be painstakingly analyzed by an expert before its clues unmask the correct molecular structure.

Collaborating with chemists and academic colleagues at Stanford—chiefly the geneticist and Nobel laureate Dr. Joshua Lederberg, Dr. Carl Djerassi, the organic chemist also know as the father of the birth control pill, and the computer scientist Dr. Bruce Buchanan—Feigenbaum wrote a series of heuristic rules for Dendral representing the way different molecules break down under mass spectroscopy. These rules function as if/then rules, but because they are steeped in chemical terminology, they are not all that comprehensible to the layperson. They piece together all the possible and unique substructures that can be inferred from the mass spectral graph. These candidate substructures are then evaluated by comparing the actual known data about them, in this instance garnered from mass spectrometry, with the predicted behavior of chemical elements. If the data compare favorably, the substructure is considered to be present; if unfavorably, it is rejected. In this way, the number of candidates is reduced to a few—possibly even one—that best explain the actual molecule at hand.

Dendral and its rules are thorough. Hundreds or even thousands of chemically plausible candidates are suggested by each unknown compound that presents itself. Often, many of these are overlooked by human chemists because the task of proposing chemical scenarios and then evaluating them is so complex and time consuming. Indeed, Dendral has been a showcase computer for expert-system technologists. It works and works well. Hooked to a mass spectrometer from which it receives data directly, it has been churning out atomic analyses with remarkable accuracy. Since its creation, Dendral has been installed in dozens of universities and industrial chemical labs worldwide. Even beyond receiving acclaim as a computer equal to most human chemists, Dendral can claim an additional virtue: It is much cheaper to run than all previously used methods for determining chemical structures. "Because Dendral knows so much about chemistry and the methods of mass spectrometry," says Feigenbaum, "and because it is so systematic in its reasoning, it can solve chemical structure problems using low-resolution spectral data which is relatively inexpensive to attain. Human chemists trying to solve these structure problems on their own in the past always had to use the more costly high-resolution instruments."

Dendral's noteworthy success led Feigenbaum to the

idea that perhaps it could be used to circumvent the nagging problem of making knowledge engineering more efficient. As Feigenbaum describes his decision, he became convinced that Dendral had "laid a foundation firm enough that it could be used to pursue the deeper and more critical study of heuristic formation itself."

Consequently, in the early 1970s, Feigenbaum began writing a program called Meta-Dendral, planned as an expert system turned inside out. Meta-Dentral was programmed to literally write its own rules describing how molecules and compounds fragment when they are studied under mass spectrometry—which Dendral itself could then use. The project was a success, producing a primitive program that worked as a knowledge engineer by the mid-1970s, and much more sophisticated programs by the end of that decade. "Meta-Dendral is a program that finds rules as opposed to solutions," explains Feigenbaum. "Dendral is an expert system that takes one mass spectrum and searches through a space of chemical molecular possibilities looking for a small set of atomic structures to explain that one spectrum. Meta-Dendral, on the other hand, takes hundreds of thousands of atomic structures and creates rules of mass spectrometry sufficient to explain that mass of data."

Basically, the only knowledge that Meta-Dendral possessed in the beginning was a set of instructions, called the generic legal syntax, for the rules it was to create. Feigenbaum and his colleagues closely studied the rules that they had written for Dendral and extracted certain common syntactical elements that all of the rules possessed. "The first and easiest common element of the Dendral rules to discern was the form of the rule," says Feigenbaum. "That is, what is contained in the initial clause and what is contained in the consequent clause." The resultant form that emerged (translated into the if/then idiom) was:

IF a particular molecular or compound configuration exists,
THEN a certain fragmentation will occur.

"We trusted this form because we had Dendral, which showed us if you put rules in that syntax the expert system would work," Feigenbaum adds. "The success of Dendral told us that chemists thought about their discipline in that form."

Less easy to discern were the separate chemical terms that would make up the rule. But after years of investigation and honing the research, Feigenbaum found five separate chemical properties that appeared in nearly every statement in Dendral: atom, bond, break, charge and charge location. These terms, then, became Meta-Dendral's vocabulary. Whenever the description of a chemical substructure was keyed into it, the computer was to examine the description for these five properties and then create a rule of mass spectrometry based on them.

Feigenbaum was successfully able to center in on and program into Meta-Dendral the one rule or formula that a knowledge engineer would use when putting together an expert system on molecular chemical analysis. This was encouraging to Feigenbaum because it proved that perhaps automating knowledge engineering was not as complicated as he at first feared. Instead of having to create a huge set of rules to define the knowledge engineer's craft, possibly one very complete rule would suffice. Of course, having Dendral to work with as a paradigm gave Feigenbaum a superb template with which to create that one rule. He well recognized that not all other knowledge-engineering expert systems would be as easy to design.

Meta-Dendral took on the task of building rules with a vengeance. Even as the first round of chemicals was being keyed into it, hundreds of rules were being output by the computer. This was exciting to the researchers but it also represented an embarrassment of riches—a windfall that could lead to a useless system. Obviously, if too many rules were generated the resultant expert system would become so cumbersome that it would be agonizingly slow. Also, it would become so fat with heuristics that there would be no way of checking which ones were being used often and accurately and which weren't. Clearly, a method of pruning the rules as they were being designed had to be instituted.

"We added a question-and-answer program into the system," Feigenbaum says, "that enabled the computer to diagnose itself after it designs each set of rules. We cut back on the number of rules as far as possible by forcing the computer to continually refer to the data, the chemical structure information, that gave rise to these rules. Every time there is a branch added to the if/then tree, it asks of that branch, 'Is nature telling me that?' Then it goes back and looks at the data, with the help of its internal question-and-answer program. If nature is not telling it what the new if/then rules are representing—perhaps some knowledge that the computer has picked up generated a mutant, inaccurate rule—then the statements are thrown out. This way we can rapidly prune down a potential rule set that could run conceivably into the millions to one much smaller that the data is definitely pointing to as necessary."

Meta-Dendral has grown in scope since the first version of it was produced in 1976. Its rules are of comparable quality to those generated by human experts collaborating with knowledge engineers and in some cases it has created totally original rules never before defined by chemists. "Meta-Dendral came up with thirty-three rules for three different classes of steroids that explained how to decipher which steroids were present in which compounds," Feigenbaum says. "These were so unique and sufficiently good that they were published in the *Journal of the American Chemical Society*, not as freaks produced by some computer but as genuine new knowledge. The computer wasn't even mentioned in the article except in a footnote."

To some, this work of Feigenbaum's may appear to be nothing more than the esoteric labor of a member of the slide-rule class. But there is a value in what he is doing that transcends technology and offers the potential for a greater understanding of knowledge and human learning techniques. Heuristics are the key to human intelligence and to the way people use knowledge. People react to information they receive by devising mental strategies to use it efficiently—this includes tagging it for instant reference and creating intricate unconscious scenarios that describe meanings and usefulness in different contexts. Meta-Dendral works in a like fashion and thus possesses one of the most sophisticated attributes of intelligence. It is a computer that designs heuristics from raw data and, basically, one simple embedded heuristic of its own.

Feigenbaum considers himself an engineer and would give short shrift to any overtones of cognitive theory in his work. His hope is to replicate Meta-Dendral in other domains—but thus far this has not been accomplished. If and when it is, it will replace the knowledge engineer and cut down the time it takes to build an expert system. To the engineers in the artificial-intelligence community, improved manufacturing efficiency in the building of artifacts would be no small accomplishment.

## Chapter 5

# LANGUAGE, LEARNING AND SCRIPTS

"Though you may hear lip service to the contrary, the average artificial-intelligence researcher doesn't really consider himself working on understanding the mind. He's a computer designer first and foremost. That's where we differ. I look to result in a theory of mind."

Speaking is Roger Schank, the chairman of Yale's computer science department, and the man who epitomizes the current wave of artificial-intelligence research. Only ten years old when the forefathers of artificial intelligence at the 1956 Dartmouth convention wedded the discipline to formal, logic-bound, brute-force programming, Schank rejects essentially all of the notions of that period. His research is an open-ended journey into how the human mind works—how intelligent thoughts are propagated and in what form memories are stored—using language and the computer as his guides.

Schank's work can be pictured surrealistically as a door with a keyhole through which can be seen another door and another keyhole through which can be seen still another door and yet another keyhole and so on. Language, according to Schank, is the key to unbolting the first door, a door that represents the outer shell of the human mind. When opened, it leads to a patchwork of vague inferences, associations and memories—the very keys to unlocking the second door, which is hiding a vast amalgam of thoughts. Understanding the nature of these thoughts is the key to unlocking the third door, and to penetrating the mind still further. With language as the entrée, the layers and mysteries of human intelligence are pared away.

"Language is the tip of the iceberg," Schank says. "It's the expression and distillation of thoughts. For instance, if I return from vacation and you ask me how it was, I know and you know that you have the tolerance for a thirty-second answer and that's all. So I can't respond with every detail of my vacation. What I have to do is take all the thoughts and memories that I've compiled about my vacation and distill it into one sentence: 'It was hot.' I use language to express, in an efficient manner, all of my thoughts. Language and thoughts are intimately weaved. And if you look at language as the tip of the iceberg, it's nice to know what the iceberg is like.

"Traditional linguists don't agree. They think that language is just its sentences—the words, the grammar, the syntax—all of its self-evident objects. They are poorly mistaken. Language is the way into the secrets of the mind. If you create a computer that understands natural language, then you have created a computer that can think, because it will naturally generate a much wider universe of thoughts, conceptions and inferences from each sentence it understands, just as humans do."

Until now, the computer, including the expert system, has not had to comprehend so-called natural languages, languages presented in the form that people speak them. Instead, the computer immediately translates our typed alphanumeric characters into digital data, the language *it* understands. And while an expert system program is not specifically tied to the zeros and ones of binary digital code, it, too, does not grasp the relevance of free text and natural languages. When communicating with people, the expert system requires only single-word or short-phrase responses to questions it asks. The expert system is not interested in the person's language per se; it is interested in the information it needs to make decisions or reach conclusions.

Schank, on the other hand, is attempting to go well beyond these computers and their programs. He speaks of designing computers that literally understand language as humans speak it, including its contextual arrangements and its most sophisticated idioms. These computers would use their language comprehension ability to generate knowledge, intelligence and unique conclusions, just as people do. Schank's theories are more than just paper tigers. He has fathered a substantial array of computers that boast tangible results to back up his ideas. Under Schank's tutelage—and using his inspiration and ideas—around thirty artificial-intelligence researchers at Yale are designing machines (and improving on them constantly) that contain the potential for a degree of intelligence not yet seen. The machines are primitive, limited and need to be coaxed, but they are nevertheless already scientific landmarks. To make artificial intelligence a reality in the fullest definition, computers will have to understand natural languages. And at Yale, the beginning of this remarkable achievement is well under way.

These accomplishments have made Schank, at a young age, a potentially formidable figure in ongoing mind and brain research, and one of the leading lights in the field of artificial intelligence. Yet he retains the trappings of an *enfant terrible.* More arrogant than likable—and when probed, more insecure than his outward arrogance would attest to—Schank has spent much of his adult life at odds with the academic establishment.

After an undistinguished undergraduate stint at Carnegie-Mellon, where he received a degree in mathematics, he nearly lost a chance for a PhD at the University of Texas in Austin because he loudly protested the school's approach to linguistics theory, calling it wildly off-target. "It was useless for my purposes—totally concerned with grammar and not the underlying meaning of the language." Later as a professor at Stanford—at the age of twenty-three—he met up with such artificial-intelligence luminaries as Edward Feigenbaum and Edward Shortliffe and took them on for their devotion to the rule-based expert systems that, as Schank puts it, "imitate human intelligence but do not simulate it."

Finally, at Yale, he gained acceptance for his approach to natural-language research and artificial intelligence. Schank's work, unlike much of the expert-system research, is not an attempt to immediately solve real-world problems and offer technological quick fixes. And this anti-"produce or perish" bias to his work is well in tune with Yale's academic philosophy. (Yale has been slow to see academia as a place where practical, not classical, learning is taught; the university was one of the last to establish a business school and, not long ago, it seriously considered dropping its medical school because its teachings were too pragmatic.)

Yet, despite his having found a home for his theories at Yale, Schank continues to rankle the establishment. He is locked in an on-again, off-again battle with the school's president, A. Bartlett Giamatti, who disagrees with Schank's business venture, Cognitive Systems, Inc., set up to market some of his earliest and most basic natural-language machines devised at Yale. Giamatti feels that teaching, research and business are an odious mix; Schank feels that that position would be "more at home in the seventeenth century."

In some ways, it is difficult to get beyond Schank's unruly image. He seems to carefully foster this persona. Though his achievements are more and more accepted as carrying significant weight, Schank remains an enigma who seems uncomfortable, even threatened, by his own research and the possibility that it might not in the end bear enough fruit. Although on one hand he freely says that his goal is to discover a true theory of the mind, to interviewers he is often combative, and seems impetuous and defensive when asked to offer interim conclusions based on his work to date.

He instead offers flippant responses, hiding his feelings, sounding afraid of being attacked if he took on the cloak of a legitimate scientist with serious aims. Sitting in his office at Yale, a reconverted cement shell enveloped by the aged

Gothic buildings and quads, his thoughts tumble forth in free associations, as if he were taking us on a roller-coaster ride. Sentences begin slowly at first, then his delivery picks up, and the words become almost too fast to understand until they descend to a conclusion. Leaning back in a reclining chair he says with an anxious laugh: "I have no real view of the mind. I don't know how the brain works. That's only an agenda item. We may never know how it works. Or we might think we know because one of our computers proved something and we may be worlds away from the truth. Either way, it will be many years before any conclusions can be made."

Schank impudently lashes out against his university colleagues in artificial intelligence and other disciplines, employing simplistic caricatures that seem incongruous coming from one who spends most of his time searching for unique human mental traits and skills. "I don't get along with others in academia because I am not the typical intellectual, not a part of the club. I like rock music. My relationship with my children is almost entirely physical. I am not the unphysical, distant and mindbound academic that they want me to be."

But despite this public image of being above the fray, those who work with Schank in creating intelligent machines describe him as a brilliant beehive of activity who is able to see the simple in the most complex. "He has an amazing intuition, unlike almost any other human being I've ever met," says Edward Hoevy, a South African graduate student who is teaching computers to translate sentences between German and English. "There are very few people like him who can look at the human mind and describe the reasons and pathways that led the human to a particular conclusion or action. He can go down inside the mind, pull up the essential, and create a skeleton that can be filled in by further research. Philosophy has been looking at the mind, trying to understand it, for thousands of years and look how far it's gotten—sixteen flavors of existentialism. Schank using the computer is finally creating a model of it."

At the center of Schank's theory of natural language is the script. Schank developed the idea of language scripts with Yale psychologist Robert Abelson in the mid-1970s. By "script," Schank means a standard sequence of events that is repeated frequently enough for people to remember it as a related whole, as one would recall the story line of a play. It is a fixed chain of occurrences (with some slight variations) that we have become familiar and comfortable with. Put another way, the script is essentially a human memory compartment in which we store predictable day-to-day scenarios.

For instance, consider the restaurant script, a set of ordered general expectations that we have stored in our minds which describes what happens when we go to a restaurant:

*A maître d' seats you;*
*the waitress hands you a menu and takes your drink order;*
*the waitress brings you your drink, takes your dinner order and you hand her your menu;*
*the waitress serves your dinner;*
*you eat;*

*the waitress takes your dessert order;*
*the waitress serves your dessert;*
*you eat dessert;*
*the waitress brings your bill;*
*you pay the bill.*

This script, like the thousands of others we have formed, remains tagged in a portion of our minds, waiting to be used as knowledge or be attached to a new thought or event.

Because of the presence of this script, one person speaking to another need only mention a few of the elements in it to signal his listener that the restaurant script is being used. The listener, then, having accessed the script containing the bulk of his restaurant experiences, can infer what the speaker leaves out. One sentence spoken causes a whole range of thoughts to leap into the listener's mind—thoughts that were never even mentioned. Inferences are generated from a few words.

As an example, if an acquaintance—call him James—said, "I went to a restaurant and ordered one of their new three-quarter-pound hamburgers. It was far too filling," you would infer the elements of the story he left out. James didn't say that he ate the hamburger, but you intuitively know that he did; he didn't say whether he paid his bill before he left, but you assume that he did. This is because you can hold James's story up against your restaurant script and compare it to your expectations.

Without the additional information inferred from the restaurant script, James's statement would be confusing at best. For one thing, you would probably be wondering how

James knew the hamburger was filling because, taking his story literally, he never mentioned that he ate it.

This one simple Schank notion—that scripts represent vehicles for information and knowledge and are, therefore, the fulcrum for our understanding of language—is the key element that shifted artificial-intelligence work at Yale into higher gear. Memory (because without it we could not build or use scripts), language, the generation of inferences and information understanding are cemented together in Schank's theories, with the script acting as the glue. Consequently, the Yale researchers assert that for a computer to communicate using natural language it has to understand the world—be it a limited domain or an unlimited one—in which it exists; and to understand, it too has to have a series of scripts as the backbone for its knowledge. Otherwise, playing the role of the listener in the example above, the computer would tell James that he could not possibly have known the hamburger was filling because he didn't eat it.

Looking from the center of his model of the mind—knowledge—to its outermost shell—language—Schank assumed that if he could program information into a computer about real-world events in the form of scripts, then it would, if his theory were true, understand language. In the mid-1970s this was still academic wishful thinking. It would take a few years before Schank could prove it on a computer. But when he finally did, he could be said to have simulated intelligence in a machine.

But before his computer projects could become fully realized, a second important notion—one that grew out of scripts—had to be formulated. This notion relates to the ability of knowledge to build on and replicate itself. According to Schank, the sum of what a person knows is considerably more than the individual pieces of knowledge that created it.

As Schank describes it, the script is really only a static memory-and-information packet. By joining forces with various mental devices, however, it becomes a much more useful and flexible factor in the learning equation. One device that people often use is called learning by failed predictability. It works this way: When any expectation in a script is not met, new knowledge is automatically created. In essence, the very fact that the unexpected has occurred jolts us to a higher level of intelligence. As a hyperbolic example, imagine a boy born to an isolated tribe in a desert environment where he does not see any rain for the first five years of his life. His weather script would read, "Hot, sunshine daily." The boy's memory compartment on this subject, because of environmental conditions around him, would be small indeed. If, however, during his sixth year, it rained with a vengeance one day, the predictability of his weather script will have failed. The boy then sets out to carefully compare these new, uncommon weather conditions with those he has stored in his memory. In so doing, the boy learns, because the rain has infringed upon his script, that there is an additional component to weather besides sunshine. The potential for rainstorms can now be attached to his weather script as a possible, though still statistically unusual, climatic event. In short, the script—up till now only a static memory component—becomes an active memory component which the boy can use to learn from by comparing new bits of knowledge against it. Thus, by tying new information to previous expectations, greater intelligence is achieved.

The restaurant script offers a more concrete example of the power of failed predictability. Suppose the traditional restaurant script examined before turns out to have been violated recently by restaurateurs who have developed new approaches to the culinary experience. Consider the newly fashionable dining spots where patrons pay the waiters for their food at the time it is ordered, before it is prepared.

This new wrinkle, because it breaks with tradition, is confusing the first time it is confronted. For most people, used to their well-formed restaurant scripts, a central expectation (that the bill is paid at the end of the meal) will have been confounded.

How does the mind deal with this new piece of information? According to Schank, it adds this new payment scheme to the restaurant script as a secondary possibility in the script's statement concerning the way money is paid when dining out. And in doing so, it uses this one slice of information to partially recreate the overall knowledge base of a script.

"Memory and new experiences are reconstructing scripts all of the time," Schank says. "If your memory were a collection of single episodes, and not tied to a contextual device like a script, there would be no learning. This is because learning is based on comparing something new against a previous experience. When you get two experiences that can be related in this cross-contextual way—the new against the old—you put them together and all of a sudden you have learned something."

In short, the fact that at some restaurants we paid before eating means nothing and is a useless piece of information unless it is measured against a previous custom of payment. If we had no scripts to compare new information against, we would jerk from one experience to the next devoid of contexts within which to make judgments and inferences about our environment. The accuracy and saliency of new pieces of information could never be measured. Instead, the script serves as a vehicle for evolving knowledge. Paying the restaurant bill may seem a simplistic example. But we learn about far weightier and more complex matters in much the same way, often by juggling elements of many, even hundreds of scripts.

Scripts also enable us to quantify the value of new information vis-à-vis past experiences. For instance, because we only infrequently pay before eating, that particular method of payment is stored initially as a distant secondary possibility in the restaurant script. But if it begins to happen frequently, it becomes a more distinct possibility, even to the point of becoming equal in the script to paying after eating. If paying before eating becomes the norm for all restaurants, then that concept takes a central place in the restaurant script, and in the process the original expectation is discarded.

To play this scenario out further, if the new became the norm, what would then become of the discarded original notion of paying after eating? It would be placed in a separate corner of the mind, Schank says, to remain as a memory of earlier years, to be tinged vividly with nostalgia or to fade away and be forgotten as it loses its importance.

Interestingly, our reactions to comedy and much of literature and film are based on this same mental process whereby the unexpected clashes against the expectations lodged in our scripts. Humor, for instance, depends first on relating our own experiences to the story being told. Internally, we access the series of scenarios, the scripts, that describe how the story would unfold if it followed predictable paths. Ultimately, when the punch line comes, we find it funny because it provides an unexpected conclusion to the story—a twist in language or action that is amusing simply because it jars us away from our preset expectations. Abbott and Costello's classic "Who's on first" routine is a prime example of this, with its brilliant plays on some of the simplest words of the language, putting new meanings on them by turning common pronouns into proper nouns. It also shows how important a role language plays in our memories and expectations, a notion that Schank is particularly comfortable with.

Beyond offering a prime example of failed predictability at work, the restaurant payment episode provides the first glimpse into how Schank has taken his theory of scripts and used its central components as knowledge-building devices in a computer. The device he uses is called the programming demon, known also as the memory demon. This device is based on the physical means, according to Schank, that people use to juggle and quantify the information in their scripts.

It works this way: After dining at the fictitious Pay First Eatery once or twice, or even hearing about the way it operates, a person's restaurant script is altered so that the next time it is examined it contains two distinct possibilities for considering how restaurants are paid for their services.

The two possibilities, with a probability statistic attached, are the script's demons.

Demon 1: When I eat at a restaurant, 90 percent of the time I pay the bill *after* I eat.
Demon 2: When I eat at a restaurant, 10 percent of the time I pay the bill *before* I eat.

The demons serve as two coexistent expectations of the script until they can be separately accepted or rejected from further consideration.

If someone tells you, "When I went to the restaurant last night, I was shocked to see, when I finally got the bill, that the little bit I ate cost ninety-five dollars," Demon 2 is discarded. Though the speaker's language was somewhat ambiguous, by pure inference you can eliminate the irrelevant demon. On the other hand if someone tells you, "The restaurant tab was so expensive that after paying it, I lost my appetite and didn't eat a thing," Demon 1 is let go, by similar inferencing. Moreover, if the time of payment cannot be inferred from succeeding statements, and is probably irrelevant to the story being told, you accept, because of the statistical frequencies attached to each of the demons, that Demon 1 contains the accurate assumption.

Schank and his colleagues like to point out a sentence that enables one to actually feel the use of demons at work. Say the following sentence to yourself slowly (and think about each word as you say it):

*The old man's glasses . . . contained sherry.*

Some people, having no "glasses demons" attached to their scripts about old men, assume eyeglasses are the subject of the sentence and are momentarily confused by its last two words. On the other hand, other, less literal-minded people have two relevant "glasses demons" in their scripts about old men, and they come into play as the first four words of the sentence are spoken:

Demon 1: An old man can possess eyeglasses.
Demon 2: An old man can possess drinking glasses.

And with the last two words of the sentence, these listeners discard Demon 1.

Language, Schank's work shows, is indeed a window of some clarity into the mind. A whole set of thoughts, new knowledge and previously repressed ways of viewing the world around us can erupt from a sentence that would be totally cryptic and useless to a machine unaware of its environment.

"Language has a way of introducing lots of concepts subliminally," Schank says. "This occurs because it attaches itself to scripts which are an already codified set of information that is associated in the mind with a particular domain or event. Without the script, inferences about a statement would be spewed out willy-nilly. There would be no foundation on which to build accuracy into the learning process. The script allows the inference process to be constrained and is therefore useful as a generator of specific knowledge."

Schank's theories of scripts and demons offer powerful and unique ideas about learning and memory. But had he not had computers on which to test them, they would have remained just graceful ideas, interesting but unproven, about how the mind and brain operate. For the activist Schank, that would be far from enough. Fortunately, his computer expertise enabled him to put his theories to the test, to prove concretely whether his notions were sound. While Schank claims that his main aim is to extend his model of the mind, a by-product of his work is that he has taken artificial intelligence—and natural-language work in the discipline—quite a few steps closer to fruition.

Having constructed an original set of ideas about knowledge and its retention, Schank never considered using the formal programming and constraints of if/then rules to prove it. Instead, he set out to teach computers about the real world through scripts. Scripts, he hoped, would be used by computers just as humans use them; that is, as motivators for building knowledge. He assumed that if his notion was indeed correct—that humans learn by processing language, continually breaking down and building up their embedded scripts in response to new information received—then a computer should be able to emulate the process. If his idea was incorrect, the computer would fail to learn and would exhibit no discernible intelligence.

Schank's ideas have thus far met their tests well. Consider the spate of computer programs being written at Yale that learn by being fed a steady diet of information about a restricted subject—be it diplomatic relations, auto accidents, the weather, horse racing or football, to name a few. Using information on these topics that is typed into the computer with natural free text, these programs are able to answer questions, provide summaries or predict future events in their domains. Essentially, each of these computers possesses one or more basic scripts that allow it to build or reconstruct knowledge as it receives new pieces of information.

"The IPP program is probably our most evolved result thus far in watching a computer actually think, to some degree," says Stephen Slade, vice-chairman of the computer department at Yale. "All it knows about is terrorism and all it reads is UPI wire stories on terrorism."

IPP, for Integrated Partial Processing, was developed at Yale in the late 1970s by Michael Lebowitz, who is now a professor at Columbia University. Before he closed the books on IPP, Lebowitz spent three years—eighteen months of research and eighteen months of programming—cramming five hundred wire service stories or pieces of text on terrorism into the program's memory. "What Lebowitz set out to do is build a program that can read a story in natural language, generalize it into its component parts, and then create a memory structure or script from these generalizations," says Edward Hoevy, the Yale graduate student. "This is so that when it reads a second story, it gets reminded of what it already knows about the subject by accessing its script, just as humans do. The program also has to, as it's registering the new information, update the knowledge it already has in memory and create more sophisticated and comprehensive memory structures or scripts to rely on in the future."

When IPP was ready to read its first story, it already had certain basic knowledge—a group of terrorist scenarios—programmed into it using a conceptual, nonbinary programming language. Lebowitz embedded this knowledge in order to equip the machine with the amount of information most intelligent people amass with no effort, purely as a result of being functioning human beings in an information-intensive society. What the computer knew about terrorism before it dissected its first story on the subject was not much different from what a reasonably curious teenager, perhaps, would glean from a simple awareness of the world around him—before he, also, read his first terrorist story seriously.

The fact that Lebowitz had to make very careful decisions about what knowledge to program into the computer at the inception of his research points to the crucial difference that will always separate the human being from the computer. People are intelligence gatherers, even when we are not aware of it. We unwittingly create memory structures and knowledge bases in our minds about a dazzling variety of subjects, seemingly by pure osmosis. A computer, on the other hand, always has to be force-fed the foundations of its knowledge. No matter how intelligent a computer may appear to be at the height of its development, it will never create knowledge out of whole cloth at its first stages. The efficacy of the initial information programming will always be the key to its ultimate success as an intelligent machine. By contrast, people can take many wrong turns, misunderstand concepts and facts and still finally end up with a great amount of knowledge about a subject.

The scenario that IPP initially received was essentially a schematic for a budding and immature terrorist script. It looked like this:

```
IN AN ACT OF TERRORISM THERE IS
  AN ACTOR
    THE TERRORIST
  THAT
    ATTACKS
      KILLS;
      WOUNDS; OR
      KILLS AND WOUNDS
  WHO?
    A MEMBER OR MEMBERS OF THE ESTA-
    BLISHMENT
  WHERE?
    AT THE LOCATION OF DISPUTE.
```

As you can see, in sharp contrast to the static and limited if/then rules used in traditional expert systems, the natural-language researchers at Yale are programming whole concepts and thoughts—real-world scenarios—into their computers. These scenarios or scripts are flexible because they are general enough to shift in many new directions, depending upon what incoming information they receive.

Unlike the expert systems, they can intelligently react whether the incoming information supports their conclusions or violates them.

The general components of IPP's script—an Actor that Attacks a Victim—become the computer's means to intelligence whenever specific names and actions are attached to these components. The specifics are gathered from news text. To follow IPP through this process of attaching useful meanings to the general concepts it already knows, consider a UPI story with a lead like this: IRA GUERRILLAS AMBUSHED A MILITARY PATROL IN BELFAST KILLING ONE BRITISH SOLDIER AND WOUNDING ANOTHER.

The Actor is a group in this case, the IRA guerrillas. This one phrase enables the computer to infer at least two pieces of new knowledge, which it will remember for future use. It now knows, first, that the IRA is a terrorist group. This is because the computer is obsessed with terrorism; all actors, it assumes from the limited range of its knowledge, must be terrorists. Secondly, the computer concludes that the word *guerrillas*, because it coexists in this phrase with the acronym IRA, can be linked from here on in with terrorism.

The Attack in this case is an "ambush." The word *ambush* can now be added to IPP's personal dictionary as meaning a type of terrorist violence that leads to death or wounding.

The Who? or Member of the Establishment is a military patrol. Subsequently, each time the term military is read, it will be seen to represent the establishment.

The Where? is Belfast. A new knowledge link is created. In the future, any time the program sees the location Belfast in a dateline or a sentence it will immediately assume that the terrorists involved are IRA activists.

The rest of the UPI lead serves to confirm or discard the three script demons lurking in the terrorist scenario relating to the outcome of the attack.

Demon 1: The attack (ambush in this case) kills the member of the establishment.

Demon 2: The attack (ambush in this case) wounds the member of the establishment.

Demon 3: The attack (ambush in this case) wounds and kills members of the establishment.

Demon 3 is confirmed by the text, while the other two demons are discarded. Because it is at the moment limited to having read only this one lead, IPP now assumes that in most terrorist actions the victims are both killed and wounded. Thus far, that is the extent of its knowledge of the world. This gross generalization will, of course, be proved wrong by subsequent UPI reports and then be forgotten.

Further, the use of the term soldier in the sentence as a direct reference to the previously identified victim (the military patrol) allows the program to link soldier to both the Establishment and the military for future reference. IPP now understands that the British soldier is a possible and predictable victim in IRA terrorist attacks.

"This one story allows IPP to revise its script with a raft of generalizations that enable it to understand better the next terrorist story it reads," Hoevy says. "It took the computer five seconds to digest the UPI lead, and order it into separate parts that make sense to its script-based expectations."

In IPP's "mind" its updated script would look something like this:

```
IN AN ACT OF TERRORISM THERE IS
  AN ACTOR
    THE TERRORIST
    THE GUERRILLA
      THE IRA
  THAT
    ATTACKS
    AMBUSHES
      KILLS;
      WOUNDS; OR
      KILLS AND WOUNDS (strongest
        probability)
  WHO?
    A MEMBER OF THE ESTABLISHMENT
      MILITARY PATROL
      BRITISH SOLDIER
  WHERE?
    AT THE LOCATION OF DISPUTE
      BELFAST (site of IRA terrorism).
```

The script, now made more formidable by specific knowledge, begins to take shape as a multitiered hierarchy, each succeeding level supported by the power of more accurate and measurable knowledge. Information about terrorists of every ilk subsequently claims respective compartments in IPP's memory, to be accessed and considered as programmed demons until proven relevant or irrelevant to the particular UPI article being considered.

With each successive story it reads, IPP's understanding of terrorism is augmented by its own conclusions, drawn from the UPI reports, not those written by a programmer. And as the articles become more complicated, the computer is faced with—and succeeds at—generating accurate inferences from truly ambiguous statements, something that clearly denotes the presence of intelligence. Consider the following UPI text, read by IPP after about twenty previous stories:

BELFAST—A disgruntled Catholic gunman shot and killed a part-time policeman at a soccer match and escaped through the crowd to a waiting getaway car.

IPP first searches through its memory for the implications of a Belfast dateline. It finds a link that identifies the city as the location of many IRA terrorist activities. By reaching that one conclusion—that the IRA is the actor in this scenario—all of the other possible terrorists it has previously read about (the actor demons) are discarded as players in this particular news story.

A reordering of its script, based on this initial IPP inference, follows. Like falling dominos, all memory associations that are allied to any terrorist actions other than the IRA's are discarded. Only events or characters linked to the IRA are retained as predictable actions of varying degrees for this news story.

This pruning of its internal script represents a method of efficient information processing analogous to how the brain functions. Rather than sort through an entire memory bank just to eventually use five or even ten facts, data that are clearly irrelevant are first eliminated; only applicable information is accessed.

Asked to explain the above UPI lead, IPP responded: "A member of the IRA, allied to the Catholic cause, attacked a member of the establishment, a policeman, killing him." Though the news text neither mentioned the IRA (it called the terrorist "a disgruntled Catholic gunman") nor identified whether the policeman represented the pro-British establishment, in all probability IPP's assumptions in this case are right. In fact, they are assumptions that most people would also make confronted with this UPI report. For better or worse, quite fallible generalizations, often the result of inferences based on past experiences, are the foundation of human mental skills—and IPP's. In fact, it is precisely because our reasoning process is assumption-based that we are able to deal with new information in an economical fashion. If, instead, we felt it necessary to nail down perfect interpretations of information—interpretations with no remaining assumptions or questions—before proceeding to analyze subsequent pieces of data, we would be rendered mentally incapacitated by our own attempt to think.

One part of IPP's analysis of this UPI lead, though, struck the Yale artificial-intelligence researchers as flimsy and representing a lack of intelligence: its linking the Catholic cause to the IRA terrorist movement. Of course, the computer was accurate in its assessment of the Irish imbroglio. But the researchers were dissatisfied because they felt that IPP was speaking from a position of nothing more than ignorance about this aspect of the story.

IPP understands terrorism in black and white terms and sees it as nothing more than a crossfire of actors and victims. It does not understand motives, be they based on religious differences, territorial struggles or jingoism. Thus the computer, Yale researchers perceptively concluded, was merely repeating words by rote, taken from earlier news stories, when it linked the Catholics and their cause with the IRA. IPP did not know in any sense what Catholic meant; it had no historical or holistic understanding of religious squabbles. A subtle point, perhaps, but a significant one because it shows that what might appear as intelligence—in a machine or a person—can be the babble of a moron. With some dismay, the researchers pointed to this as an example of how a computer—like the 1956 Logic Theory Machine—can mimic human cognitive abilities without, in fact, possessing any.

Interestingly, a bright child would probably make the same inference about religious motives, also without a deeper understanding of the Protestant/Catholic conflict in

Ireland. But if he or she were interested, the child would know enough to ask an adult the reasons why Catholicism was the center of the dispute in Ireland. Additionally, the child outpaces the computer because even at a young age he or she has an unlimited number of scripts—not only the terrorist one—on which to attach the adult's response.

The IPP developers, though, were not dealing with the mind of a seeking child, but only the memory of an incurious and un-goal-oriented machine. So they had a decision to make because of the computer's moment of ignorance. They could expand IPP's memory base to include an explanation of why those of different religions historically often fail to get along, or they could simply keep the computer in the dark.

They opted for the former. But to avoid wasting the not unlimited memory space of the computer with reams of tangential information about religious strife, they programmed only the facts of religious discord as they related to the Irish struggle.

This was not the only time that the Yale researchers would face a question about religion from IPP. Having armed the computer with only a very limited "religious prejudice in Ireland" script, it was predictable that the computer would come up ignorant again when it hit upon the underlying causes of terrorism in Lebanon. This time the IPP researchers decided against informing the computer.

Our curious child, on the other hand, would have an easier time comprehending the sad logic motivating the actions in the torn Mideast nation. This is because he or she would be able to attach the activities of the Shiite and Druse

Moslems, the PLO and all the less-heralded sects in the region to the script he created while learning about what is propelling the actions of the IRA and the British.

Nevertheless, despite its shortcomings, IPP's ability to learn from inferences is a significant landmark in artificial intelligence. What it means is that a computer can actually create unique information from within itself and far surpass the verbatim regurgitation of a series of rules programmed from without, which is the hallmark of traditional expert systems. Indeed, IPP showed in the one example given here the use of an elegantly creative thought process—the association of ambiguous statements to arrive at an original statement of fact. This is a primary step in the evolution of an intelligent mind.

Of course, such creative inferencing can also lead to some embarrassing misinterpretations, as when a precursor of IPP called FRUMP, another UPI reader, sent out a message that an earthquake had occurred in the United States. FRUMP, however, breaking with its habit, did not report the location and scale of the quake and how many casualties were involved. This alerted the Yale researchers that something was amiss. The researchers burrowed through FRUMP's reading diet for the day looking for clues as to how it reached its conclusion that there had been an earthquake. They found what they were looking for in the pile of UPI texts when they saw the headline: "Death of Pope Shakes U.S." FRUMP had clearly been overly literal.

Fortunately, errors like this are infrequent aberrations. IPP and its cohorts work so well precisely because news stories, with their who, what, when, where and how structures, are so scriptlike and literal-minded that they are ideally suited to a computer's inherent inflexibility of thought.

Mindful that the IPP approach lacks, ultimately, an easy means of leaving news texts behind, some artificial-intelligence researchers at Yale have attempted to build on the script theory in ever more creative ways. A good example is the computer called ABDUL/ILANA, designed a few years after IPP. Like a person with two minds, ABDUL/ILANA constructs both sides of an argument by picking and choosing and then joining together previously unrelated facts and memories in its script structures. In a rudimentary way, it is able to understand the positions of the adversaries. For this type of program, the Mideast debate, in which the differences of the principal antagonists are so clear-cut, was the chosen dialogue. What follows is a fragment of an ABDUL/ILANA discussion:

1) Arab: Who started the 1967 war?
2) Israeli: The Arabs did, by blockading the Straits of Tiran.
3) Arab: But Israel fired first.
4) Israeli: According to international law, blockades are acts of war.
5) Arab: Were we supposed to let you import American arms through the straits?
6) Israeli: Israel was not importing arms through the straits. The reason for the blockade was to keep Israel from importing oil from Iran.

7) Arab: But Israel was importing arms, and that's because Israel is trying to take over the Middle East.

"Statement (1) is the starting point of the argument and allows the program to choose sides," says Tina Karsberg who worked with ABDUL/ILANA while she was at Yale in the early 1980s. "The first part of Statement (2) is generated by a rule of arguments which always assumes that the opponent in the argument is responsible for any 'bad' events. The second part of Statement (2), the blockade accusation, attempts to justify the first part of the statement. The program comes to this accusation by looking through the scripts in its memory for an event in the past which has the correct actor—the Arabs—and is in the correct chronological setting, right before the '67 war."

In Statement (3) the computer, thinking as the Arab, searches through its memory to find a possible cause of the war that has the Israelis as the actors. But in Statement (4) the Israeli feeling that it has begun building up a lethal argument of its own in Statement (2) ignores the Arab claim and instead justifies Statement (2) by citing international law. The Arab is now clearly on the defensive and must argue on the Israeli's terms. ABDUL/ILANA attempts to explain the reasons, from the Arab point of view, for the blockade.

To do this, the program searches through its memory to find a mitigating warlike act, again one that occurred in the same historical period, on the part of the Israelis. At first blush, it appears to be successful. But, unfortunately for the Arab, in its zeal and desire to justify the blockade the computer selectively forgets and alters the facts to fit its argument. To wit, though it is true that Israel was importing arms from the U.S. at the time, it was not doing so through the Straits of Tiran.

"The Israeli is ready to strike paydirt now," Karsberg says. "The fascinating thing is that carrying the arguments of adversaries, ABDUL/ILANA seems to take on the kinds of emotional baggage that debating evokes in humans. First in Statement (5) it misrepresented a fact to make a point as the Arab. And now in Statement (6) as the Israeli it goes on to weaken the Arab's justification for the blockade by—can it be delightedly?—shoving the actual reason for it in the Arab's face."

So with the Arab now battered and backed into a corner, the program in Statement (7) shifts the focus away from the inopportune question of whether or not the blockade was justified. It instead raises the far more fundamental and deep-seated issue of the possible expansionist habits of Israel. It was a calculated and good move by ABDUL/ILANA, because as the dialogue continues, the Israeli, baited by the Arab's statement, responds to this new level of argument. The debate turns down a different path, one more treacherous for the Israeli.

ABDUL/ILANA underscores that a computer can be made to have an intelligent discussion by creatively associating and juxtaposing information it has stored in separate memory compartments. Also, in a somewhat more abstract sense, ABDUL/ILANA appears to take on the human emotional characteristic of relishing one-upmanship in argument. Where do emotions such as these come from, in people or machines? That issue, while too abstruse to be high on the agenda yet, is at least asked around the Yale computer department because of ABDUL/ILANA. But more important, ABDUL/ILANA, like its far more limited antecedent, IPP, is a model, the Yale researchers contend, of their concept of intelligence as the art of reconstruction; i.e., intelligent behavior does not rest on using actual memories of events or ideas in the form they are originally experienced, but rather on reconstructing unique arguments or actions from the generalizations offered by these memories.

Natural-language research is central to artificial intelligence. Ultimately, it will afford computer users the luxury of having the machine understand them in their own native tongues and of receiving responses from the computer in similar free-form language. Perhaps more importantly, though, the use of natural language is now opening up layers of intelligence in computers that, ironically, were constrained by the previously popular notion that communicating with computers in their own numerically-based language was the only possible approach.

But as worthy as its research would seem to be, one criticism is persistently leveled at the Yale artificial-intelligence community, especially from the builders of expert systems. It is said, and said often, that the Yale computers are dozens of years away from being put to any specific useful purposes for society at large. Schank shrugs off this argument. He prefers to clothe himself in the virtues of an abstract humanist who is interested only in constructing models of the mind in a computer. Nevertheless, the argument has some merit. Even within the ranks at Yale there is a budding backlash against the imperiousness of Schank's position.

A feeling exists among some at Yale that unless something of tangible value emerges from the university's work in artificial intelligence, federal R&D funds will become sparse and the computer project will be cut to its bare bones. These few say that prototypes of reading or thinking computers with barely the intelligence of teenagers are not needed anymore; instead, computers are needed that can use the remarkable Yale breakthroughs in machine intelligence to offer advice now to people about the most complex and crucial human domains.

This statement would seem to be grounds for a beheading at Yale, sounding as it does so opposed to Schank's position. But one of the leading voices in this camp, a graduate student named Larry Hunter, is skirting the controversy of his position by proving that the development of a Schank-influenced version of the expert system is possible. His program undertakes to show that unlike Stanford's Mycin, for example, an advisor system—as Hunter likes to call it—is within reach that is not rule-bound, but rather relies on reasoning and knowledge gained from its own experiences and memories.

The expert Hunter is modeling on a computer is Dr. Raymond Yessner of the West Haven Veterans Administration Hospital in Connecticut. His specialty is lung tumor diagnoses and pathology, a field in which he is considered one of the leading practitioners in the world. What Hunter hopes to create over the next couple of years is a computer that possesses enough of Yessner's intelligence in oncology to impart his knowledge and offer advice to less-experienced physicians and medical school students. Significantly, though, this program, because it is built on the script and not the if/then rule, will be able to learn from breakthoughs in its domain and constantly rethink its approach to clinical conditions as new information warrants.

Hunter began his work in 1983 by poring over the thousands of photographic slides Yessner has collected over decades of practice that document lung tumors of all kinds and how they assert themselves in different clinical situations. The most essential of these slides were then transferred to a videodisc plugged into the computer being programmed. "The videodisc is the computer's visual memory and its visual output," Hunter says. "It is the storehouse of information—almost an internal textbook—that the computer can access to explain why it reached a certain conclusion about a tumor or, alternately, that it can use as historical information with which to reach certain conclusions. Think of it as the computer's base of experiences in lung tumor pathology. The computer will be able to retrieve any one of as many as 50,000 slides in two seconds."

The use of the slides provides the computer with flexibility. They enable the machine to associate the details of a new patient's symptoms with any similar patient condition it has stored on its slides. The computer can use this deep pool of data—combining individual slides in any way it chooses—to reach practically any conclusion. This, of course, is patently different from the rule-based expert systems, which are limited to a stringently preordered line of thinking once they break a path. As Hunter puts it: "Other expert systems have no learning abilities of their own or self-built knowledge that comes into play in individual clinical settings. Ours does."

The videodisc is but one portion of the program's embedded knowledge. The other contains a series of scripts about lung tumor pathologies and their diagnoses. To write them, Hunter has been probing Yessner, determining his heuristics for treating patients in an innumerable variety of situations. Working in the capacity of knowledge engineer, Hunter divines how Yessner arrives at a diagnosis, converts it into a roster of generalized logical steps and programs this into the computer. The difference, though, between Hunter's work and that of the programmer of the common expert system is that the Yale graduate student is primarily concerned with devising general statements, like the "Actor Attacks Victim" scenario in IPP, with no inherent data attached; he is not at all interested in a catalogue of information-bound rules.

"We are listening and watching Yessner reach conclusions," Hunter says, "especially the way a new case reminds him of a previous case and the way he then reconstructs this reminder into a new conclusion. This is like watching him in the very act of accessing a script and using it to infer new knowledge. What we want is to do cognitive modeling of Yessner's reasoning process and his scripts; we do not simply want to list the rules of every situation he encounters. We want the computer to understand how to reason the way he does so that it can make its own rules."

Though this work is, of course, directly related to the ground-breaking Yale design for IPP, there is a basic difference between the two computers. IPP essentially learned from the bare bones of a very basic terrorist script to make its own broader generalizations and then its own specific assumptions. Hunter's program, instead, is being embedded with a large number of Yessner's scripts. At least in its initial stages of learning, it is left much less to its own devices.

"We felt that an oncology program could not learn from scratch," Hunter explains. "It would take much too long. The domain is too difficult and complicated. What we are trying to input though is not all of Yessner's knowledge, just all of his good reasoning instincts. The pure knowledge that the program will hold when it is given its first real run-through is no more than a first-year oncology intern would know."

Hunter hopes to have his oncology program ready by 1986. The computer is expected to react using the typical Yale artificial-intelligence protocol. First, the physician will input a patient's symptoms and the computer will search through its memory for similar cases (some to be located on its videodisc and others lodged in its internal program). It will then access the scripts Yessner used when treating these earlier cases. It will discard or approve the Demons in the scripts as their worthiness is determined. Finally, it will arrive at a series of assumptions concerning diagnosis and lines of treatment and then output these conclusions to the physician. Moreover, if its conclusions are wholly original, they can be stored as new scripts; as new knowledge that can be relied on in the future. Alternately, if the conclusions are those it has reached before, the computer will see them as further strengthening the statistical accuracy of the scripts involved.

Importantly, because the computer is based on Schank's

central notion that language is a key to thought and learning, it will understand the underlying conceptual meaning of the words and phrases it is handling. This means that physicians communicating with the machine will be able to input information in natural human text, and avoid using the stilted language requirements of a Mycin dialogue.

The work at Yale is proceeding apace, but it is pursued in an academic conclave of "pessimistic realists," as one insider dubbed himself and his colleagues. Nobody at Yale expects to create a model of the mind on a computer even in the near future, so unless Hunter's research proves workable in the real world, there could be a crisis of confidence—and more importantly, a crisis of funds—at the university's artificial-intelligence center.

"There have been only thirty years of artificial intelligence—most of them wasted—so of course we're still in a nascent state," Schank says. "The problem is that we live in a world where scientists must live in the real world and produce. Scientists no longer, unfortunately, have the leisure of living in the ivory towers away from public pressures. It's thus hard for artificial intelligence researchers to resist the temptation to say that it will all be here tomorrow, that artificial intelligence will be achieved before you turn around again."

Schank shrugs his shoulders. Returning is the self-portrait he likes to paint of the innocent under inordinate burdens—of the man who should be left alone to work or his genius will be buried.

"It seems that the only way the public can understand what we are doing is it's either impossible and quixotic—a waste of money—or it's already here."

## Chapter 6

# TWENTY QUESTIONS —ORGANIZING A DISORGANIZED UNIVERSE

On July 4, 1981, Kenji Urata was stabbed repeatedly and then crushed to death by an irrepressible robot in the Akashi, Japan, factory of Kawasaki Heavy Industries. It was a quiet, warm and humid morning, bathed in thick sheets of fog. The automobile and motorcycle facility seemed eerily still. There were few people at work and the factory was enveloped by the incessantly high-pitched, stainless steel sound of a variety of robots gliding purposefully up and down the corridors, delivering parts and counting inventory as they docked with other machines.

The thirty-seven-year-old Urata is remembered as an exceedingly conscientious plant repairman, who watched the workings of the Kawasaki factory with a keen, responsible eye. This trait would turn out to be a fatal virtue. According to his coworkers, Urata noticed from a distance that one of the machines in the automobile gear sector was out of kilter. He entered the restricted zone to attempt a quick repair without shutting down the factory. The rest of the machines, including the shuttling robots, continued to work.

Urata got so engrossed in his repair job, which apparently took a lot longer than he expected it to, that he failed to notice the approach of one of the robots. With his back to the oncoming robot and his attention fixed on the gear driller he was adjusting, the worker was easy prey. The robot pummeled him over and over again before crushing him to death as it tried, vainly at first, to reach the gear driller, its destination.

The Urata incident became a worldwide cause célèbre, setting off some irrational headlines about the imminent takeover of our workplaces (and eventually our overall society) by fiendish, demonic robots intent on machine hegemony. It led to calls for limiting robotic development as fervent as those that were being made against gene splicing.

This attitude is, of course, misguided and uninformed. It assumes that robots possess the ability to consciously plan, act on their own and pursue goals they deem beneficial to their group. Quite to the contrary, the robot in the Urata accident and all of its counterparts built until then—and up to now for that matter—are nothing more than dumb, blind devices with no characteristics that approach people's mental skills or, indeed, those of any living beings. And therein lies their most severe threat to society. The plain fact is that the fault for Urata's death can be placed squarely on the inherent stupidity and blindness of the Kawasaki plant robot.

When artificial-intelligence researchers talk about their

work in robotics, they stress their philosophical disdain for the kind of engineering that produces the growing number of carry-and-deliver robots like the one at the Akashi Kawasaki plant. The goal of artificial-intelligence workers, instead, is to create robots that have intelligence and vision, ones that would be able to see and grasp the meaning of the danger in the Kawasaki factory and that would have taken steps to avert the accident. They view robots as potentially far more than machines of pure brawn. They conceive of robots with the capacity to think, and understand the nature of their work as well.

In the context of artificial-intelligence research, the key to smart robots is vision. Robots that can see—and that can reason and make judgments based on what they see—offer humans the possibility of having mechanical colleagues that are quickly adaptable to changing workplace situations and are able to take on those more difficult tasks that have proven to be dangerous to people. Moreover, visioned robots should make incidents like the death of Kenji Urata impossible.

Vision, combined with a powerful data base associated with sight, is the lever being used to open up arteries of cognition in the robot. But robots, of course, are to possess more than intelligence; they will also be moving, mechanical devices. Fully outfitted, they will have useful arms with sensors and grippers for touching and lifting objects, as well as some means of getting around in environments cluttered with obstacles, be it with the wheels common today or the automated legs now in the planning stages.

Advances in mechanical limbs are central on the agenda of robotics research today. But as artificial-intelligence researchers see it, this is the province of design engineers. They compare the robot's metallic latticework of sensors, pincers, legs and wires, and how they are manipulated, to the circuitry and components of the autonomic nervous system in humans and animals. Using them correctly does not require intelligence, just coordination.

The movements of our hands, legs and muscles, our constructive, well-planned maneuvers, are often fueled by unconscious reactions to what we *see;* they are the result of involuntary conclusions and interpretations our brains have made based on what our vision system tells us. The bedrock of people's intelligence in industrial or other physical-labor environments is lodged in sight. And for that very reason, artificial-intelligence researchers are devoting themselves primarily to creating paradigms of machine vision perception.

A robot with full-fledged vision perception, including the ability to process information based on sight, would be able to work the complete range of industrial jobs and shift among them freely as becomes necessary. It would take potentially harmful tasks away from people, such as cleaning up nuclear waste or hazardous chemical spills; descending mine shafts to dig for coal; and even scavenging the ocean floor for minerals, food or materials lodged in sunken ships.

Machine vision has already reached the point where robots can consistently recognize two-dimensional, black-and-white objects, but only if they are almost completely unobscured by neighboring objects and contrast sharply with their backdrops. This is a wide improvement over the earlier generation of sightless robots, but well behind what is needed for them to become useful in industrial environments. Accounting for the somewhat tardy progress in vision perception is the fact that sight is the most difficult human ability to transfer onto the computer. This is because, unlike language understanding or the ability to think heuristically, both of which could be labeled purely human internal mental attributes stemming directly from the evolution of our consciousness, vision requires a far more intimate and exacting give-and-take with the external world.

The way people see can be described as the art of organizing a disorganized universe. As such, vision represents a significant exception to the law of entropy. Our eyes are bombarded by a multitude of images as we scan the world around us. Yet our brains, with uncanny ease, elect to see only the most stable and secure elements of these images, those that lead to accurate recognition, and reject the rest. We enforce a stability on what could be an overpoweringly chaotic environment.

"Our minds are constantly simplifying the complexities of what we see," says Whitman Richards, a professor of psychology at the Massachusetts Institute of Technology and a longtime student of human vision. Richards is now working closely with those at the Artificial Intelligence Lab on the Cambridge campus to develop some far-reaching vision-perception theories and machines. "There are a whole group of possibilities in every scene we look at, but we cannot consider them all or we would be incapable of action. The purpose for seeing or identifying an object, when you break it down, is not a complex one. All we care about are the answers to certain simple questions: Will it fit in our hands? Is it light enough to carry? Is it stable? Is it a porcupine? Since what we want to do with this visual information is inherently simple, the questions we ask should be simple. We don't need to see everything at once."

During every moment of observation, from when we first scan a scene to when we make a judgment about what it is, we break the scene down into exceedingly small components. Our eyes dart like skipping stones from one element to another, taking in the most important facts about their shapes, colors, distances and textures. Our brains, in similar fashion, dance from one conclusion to the next, testing hypotheses and deductions in nanoseconds to build up a useable description of the scene. Gradually, our minds wind down and we go from being overactive sightseers to being satisfied residents in that universe. For a physiological illustration of how we constantly simplify complex environments in order to see them, consider the fact that at the instant people make final judgments about what their eyes are seeing, as few as a thousand neurons may be firing. This compares quite dramatically to the firing of millions of neurons related to sight upon first making visual contact with a scene.

At the core of our human ability to understand what we see so readily and with such little difficulty is the fact that we have stored in our minds amazingly complete and well-referenced models of our environments. These models are cross-indexed and tagged from so many different possible angles that people can distinguish even the most extensive variations an object takes on and can see through even the most impressive camouflage.

Take the shadowed, distant face that appears in a bus window for a fleeting two or three seconds as the vehicle rides by some thirty feet away at thirty-five miles an hour. Most people would barely remember actively discerning any facial features at the moment of sight or recall ever seeing the rider from that exact angle or viewpoint, yet they could most likely identify the bus rider.

Or take a friend, who as long as you have known him, has worn a beard, a toupee and glasses. You can be shown a picture of him clean shaven, bald and without glasses, and be possibly deceived about his identity at first sight. But as you explore the picture from all angles, gradually some feature of your friend that is invariant and fits a portion of your model of him comes into view and he is identifiable.

"Images are inherently ambiguous," says Robert Bolles, a senior researcher at the Stanford Research Institute's Artificial Intelligence Center in Palo Alto, California. "But people have very strong models to work from to make those images unambiguous."

Researchers feel that there are two central components of human vision that have to be represented in a computer for it to see. First, the computer must have a way to break scenes down into their simplest and most important segments while discarding the less relevant and perhaps more complex elements; secondly and concurrently, it must have useful and strong visual models, similar to people's, that it can access for object recognition. Nearly all of the robotic sight research bearing fruit attempts to determine exactly how these two visual attributes work and how they can be successfully transferred onto the computer.

An excellent example is the impressive and painstaking research into robotic vision occurring at SRI. SRI is an independent, nonprofit research agency, once a part of, but now divorced from, Stanford University. Well backed by federal government and corporate funds, it has an extensive artificial-intelligence group with fifteen researchers working on machine vision, fifteen working on natural languages and five investigating and developing expert systems. In addition, a separate robotics laboratory houses five researchers who are investigating the mechanics of sight. The vision research at the agency is generating some of the greatest interest from the corporate sector. Over twenty-five companies are sponsoring its work in this field.

Of all the vision-perception research at SRI, the most unique is that of Robert Bolles and Ronald Cain. These two men have a combined fifteen years at the Palo Alto think tank, all spent on creating robotic sight. Their current work involves teaching computers with video-camera or laser eyes to identify partially covered or shadowed three-dimensional objects from a bin stacked with metal parts. This is an ambitious leap. The farthest point anybody has come to date in machine vision is the ability to see totally unoccluded objects that are two-dimensional and black and white.

Early in their careers, Bolles and Cain took an important first step toward achieving their present success when they rejected the notions of the original vision-perception workers whose ideas were based on brute-force programming. This is, of course, similar to the denial of older theories by most current artificial-intelligence researchers in other venues of the discipline.

The initial attempts at machine vision perception were based on severely inefficient design concepts. A video camera—the robot's eye—took full-blown pictures of the object it was scanning. These pictures, resembling magnified television images, were made up of a matrix of dots called pixels. Each pixel was given a numerical grading depending upon its intensity. Perhaps a white pixel was represented by 1, a black pixel by 10 and all the grays in between from 2 through 9. Stored in the computer's memory were templates of whole objects, or in some cases just their outer edges, and a program that viewed these templates as being composed of pixels similarly scored white to black from one to ten. The computer then compared the object it was viewing to the dictionary it retained in memory and reached a conclusion as to the identity of the object, based on either complete matching of pixel gradients, or a best guess based on partial matching of the gradients.

Obviously, this brute-force method of reading all the data in memory before a result could be arrived at was time-consuming and represented a massive memory drain for the computer as its dictionary of objects grew larger and larger. Also, objects being viewed may be stacked at numerous different angles; thus computer memory models would have to be prepared for each possible angle at which the object may be facing the machine. Finally, if an object is at all obscured, the video camera will be unable to take a full-blown picture of it and the computer will never be able to adequately match the video picture it receives against its memory models; the computer would, thus, fail to recognize the object.

As one artificial-intelligence researcher put it: "The system doesn't work if a robot takes a half hour to decide whether it is going to crash into a wall in the next thirty seconds or perhaps is so confused that it never makes a decision at all. Brute-force calculation is simply inadequate for visual processing in real time."

Robert Bolles and Ronald Cain came to the same conclusion. And they were determined to create a system that eschewed the methods adopted by the early researchers. They also realized that people certainly do not use brute-force data retrieval methods to visualize scenes, any more than they use it for understanding language or planning goals. As they studied people closely, a pattern to how we see began to emerge, which didn't provide full-fledged answers but did offer a direction that the two men decided to pursue.

"How does a person find a can opener in a drawer of kitchen utensils?" Bolles asks. "If it is partially occluded by other objects, as it probably is, they recognize one of its local and distinctive features, such as a slightly curled, pointed piece of sheet metal, and then use it to hypothesize the position and orientation of the whole object. Like when I was a kid I could identify a '57 Chevy by its taillight. That one individual feature told me a lot about the whole object. Somebody could have bolted the wrong taillight onto a '58 Chevy, but over ninety-nine percent of the time I was right."

They call their work Local Feature Focus. It involves directing the computer's eyes to home in on and discern certain distinct features of an object rather than attempt to identify the entire image at first whack. Once key features of an object are recognized by the computer, so the theory goes, it can use that knowledge to identify the entire object. After a fashion, Local Feature Focus is felt to be similar to the human approach to vision. Specifically it may be compared to the way people can look at an extremely complex scene and, in order to make it more manageable and understandable, zero in on its simplest and most relevant visual segments.

To test their theory, Bolles and Cain are using car parts in three-dimensional, dumped-at-random settings. The computer is instructed to find and pick out whatever part the researchers request. The part may be partially buried in the bin or it may be camouflaged by the backdrop; the machine is expected to overcome these obstacles. So far, the research is proving to be marginally successful, but this is mostly because the computer is playing with a modest handicap: No "surprise objects" are placed before the computer's video eyes.

"The first rule about all of this is that if it is aware of what it is looking for, it is easier for the computer to find it," says Bolles. "That's a general theorem about the work. As with people, if the computer knows the parameters of the object well, then it can do a better job of finding what it is looking for."

Significantly, though, instead of the full-blown memory templates so prevalent in early machine vision systems, the Local Feature Focus computer only stores essential kernels of data about objects. These carefully chosen data enable it to deduce an object's identity in orderly steps. Therefore, the computer's eyes do not have to take complete pixel-dominated pictures of the scene it is viewing, but rather they provide bits and pieces of scanned information for the machine to digest. This scanned information can be anything from the dimensions of the object's upper plane or, breaking the object down into a combination of geometric shapes, the radii of its most prominent circles.

The job of viewing the object, not as a whole, but as a conglomeration of relevant and less relevant visual components, is left to a unique vision mechanism in Bolles and Cain's computer. Gone is the traditional video camera; replacing it is what is known as range-finding, structured-light technology. This technique uses a laser beam reflected off the surface of an object to determine the dimensions of certain geometric shapes the object possesses, shapes that are indiscernible to the naked eye.

When the computer first looks at the object, it focuses a laser beam on the object's edges to delineate its outermost boundaries. Then the beam of light is directed onto a central point of the object. The exact point where the laser beam hits the object is noted and the XYZ coordinates of that spot are measured. (Think of measuring XYZ coordinates as a way of locating an object in three-dimensional space, a way of defining it in numerical terms.) Once these XYZ coordinates are determined, the object is easier to analyze because the computer is then able to make a drawing of the object on a three-dimensional graph. The drawing can then be matched against specific visual information residing in the computer's memory.

When Bolles and Cain's computer focuses on a portion of a typical automobile casting, such as a partially hidden fender, its laser eyes will perceive the car part as a group of geometrical shapes ranging from circles to cylinders to squares to rectangles. It is possible to elicit this visual viewpoint because every three-dimensional object is a mixture of straight, concave and convex lines which can be represented as a series of two-dimensional geometrical shapes. In the case of the fender, at the central point where the laser beam intersects with the car part (its XYZ coordinate), arcs and lines are drawn which, once connected, assume these shapes. For instance, a well-curved fender may result in a computer representation dominated by thirty-two circles.

At this point the computer begins to compare these circles to information in its visual data base. Making an initial subjective judgment, the Local Feature Focus machine notices that of the thirty-two circles it has found on the fender, eighteen can be called small and fourteen can be described as large. Based on this description of the fender, the computer now considers only those automobile castings in its visual data base that are made up mostly of circles of mixed sizes. Many objects are discarded immediately at this first cutoff.

Next, the fender's fourteen large circles are measured for their exact sizes, and four of them are determined to be three inches in diameter. At this point the computer forms a secondary hypothesis, and rejects all of the models in its memory that contain no circles with three-inch diameters. Now, four possible automobile castings remain in contention. From the computer's perspective, the fender's four 3-inch circles are now the most essential visual components of the object it sees; they are the local features the computer will use for final identification purposes.

"The computer now asks what else does it know about, say, the circle in the most prominent, perhaps the centermost, position on the fender," Bolles explains. "What is this circle next to? How are its neighboring shapes distinguished? Maybe it appears that there is a particular type of plane on the inside of the circle and on its outside there is a cylindrical shape. Now of the four possible automobile parts still in consideration in the visual data base, only two have circles that fit this updated description. So the computer is down to two potential identities for this casting." The computer then asks itself exceedingly detailed questions about the circle it has decided is the most prominent one. It might try to determine the exact dimensions of the plane it found inside the circle or of the cylindrical shape poised outside of it.

"And those are the types of questions," Bolles adds, "that lead the computer to a determination of the intrinsic properties of the fender's most prominent circle. After naming these properties, the computer can proceed to its final identification of the automobile part by looking for car parts in its visual data base that correctly compare. When the computer is able to completely describe all facets of that one prominent circle, it has drawn a picture, if you will, of the Chevy's taillight, to return to my [original] analogy. As I said, from one small visual clue—a fleeting taillight—pulled out from the whole object, I can tell you whether I am looking at a '57 Chevy or a '54 Chevy."

The automobile fender under observation here by the Local Feature Focus machine has been randomly placed in a bin, much as it would appear out of the laboratory and in real-world conditions. Thus, numerous types of visual models of car parts must be placed in the computer's memory. As is the rule when people look out at their environment, one visual model will not suffice. Too many variables can change the way an object looks from one sighting to the next.

The Local Feature Focus system contains at least three

visual views in its data base for each part it is attempting to identify. One is a standard view that provides information about the entire object, assuming it is scanned unoccluded; another is called a topological view that indicates which geometrical shapes are present in each particular car part and how they are related, allowing the computer to logically and knowledgeably feel its way around the part; the third is actually a separate data base that can be accessed from many directions. Using it a computer could, for instance, receive answers to the question, "Tell me all the parts I have in memory with circles that are close to three inches in diameter."

Bolles and Cain's computer is leading machine-vision research a long way toward finally achieving true sight in a robotic device. Already the robot commonly gathers correct range data, locates prominent edges, separates the edges into straight lines and into circles and identifies most castings. It is still too slow to perform adequately in real time, however, taking as long as five to ten minutes to recognize an object. But this should change before long. SRI is readily backing this project. Thus, Bolles and Cain expect to see the Local Feature Focus machine in industrial settings soon.

"The first generation of robots with vision are so primitive that they cost industry almost more to implement than they bring back in efficiency," Ronald Cain says. "Factory foremen have to make sure that parts are separated and not obstructed so they can be seen and the background has to be such that it causes no camouflage on the parts. The vision systems are just too dumb to handle anything else. All of that costs money. Ours is an approach where we say even if you don't go to all this trouble the vision system is intelligent enough to find sufficient information about the parts on its own to identify it. Local Feature Focus is also useful if there is an enormous part being looked for and you can't allow the robot to see all of it. That type of visual search was previously unautomatable."

Nevertheless, despite the achievements, Local Feature Focus as it is now designed will always fall flat in anything but a strictly automated factory environment. Though the cumbersome, full-fledged model templates of old have been replaced in favor of slimmed-down visual data banks, the computer is still unable to generate its own inferences about what it sees. It is tied irrevocably to a limited model format and unable to break its bonds.

"Our computer knows a lot about the casting's shape, but it doesn't know anything about the casting's function," says Bolles. "So far this is admittedly low-level vision work that we are doing. We know how to find geometrical data for an object, but we have no idea how to make a computer describe what's out there above that level.

"A good example where much of this breaks down is if, say, you want to pick out a specific tree from a view of an orchard. Now people are able to scan the entire orchard, use its edges as boundaries, and then differentiate each tree. But if you're looking at the trees through a peek hole, as our computer is, how will it ever be able to separate one tree from the other. The data it receives are too limited to compare it against any useful model in its memory. There aren't enough different geometrical components to work with in that small visual space seen through a peek hole. Even people couldn't pick out what one specific tree is with only a peek hole view of it. But people are able to differentiate trees in an orchard because they simply have much larger visual contexts than computers have to call upon for vision perception."

Bolles's statement is not an idle complaint. It is justifiably heard from many computer vision researchers. Expanding the computer's visual context is the great research challenge facing artificial-intelligence workers in robotics.

Ultimate success in simple industrial arenas, judged in terms of whether a machine will be able to accurately describe its environment down to the parts in the bins and react to it correctly and intelligently, is felt to be a foregone conclusion. For this, credit should be given to the advanced state—after only two years—of projects like Bolles and Cain's. However, industrial computer vision is often recognized as a dead end. Because of its limited scope, it offers little insight into how the next step, going beyond the uncomplicated, easily modeled factory environment and endowing computers with vision in more complex real-world sites, is to be attained.

Leapfrogging industrial vision and achieving real-world computer vision is a pressing and crucial technological issue for artificial intelligence. Unless a computer is created that can see and understand an environment in the most complete sense—how objects move, feel, interact with each other, smell and sound—the robot will never be able to escape simpleton industrial tasks and perform in more difficult and dangerous sites; in short, it could not be said to truly possess the breadth of intelligence that is intrinsic to human vision.

Considering the record of artificial-intelligence robotics

work over just the past few years, the current state of vision perception research is no real cause for pessimism. Determined research is being carried out in many of the major artificial-intelligence academic centers to place machine vision skills in increasingly complex environments. One of the universities most interested in this aspect of artificial intelligence is the Massachusetts Institute of Technology, which through its well-respected Artificial Intelligence Lab, is devoting enormous amounts of research time and money to adding greater cognitive power to the immature vision perception computers of today.

The MIT lab is a hotbed of artificial-intelligence research, one of the primary centers in the country. From sparse and cramped quarters at its inception in the mid-1960s when the first primitive Digital Electric Corporation computers arrived, it has grown up into a sprawling maze of offices and computer rooms taking up three floors in a modern building across the street from the main MIT campus. Today over one hundred artificial-intelligence researchers work there, including dozens of hackers—a group of researchers without degrees or course programs but infatuated by computers and enticed by the opportunity that the university gives them to be around these machines.

The Artificial Intelligence Lab is an eclectic academic enclave, listing on its research agenda a widely scattered and creative pastiche of experimental investigations. These include the Music Cognition Program, which is studying the cognitive processes humans use when we compose, perform and listen to music; the work of Kenneth Haase, who is building an expert system that can fluidly demonstrate intelligence in more than one area, shifting between them on its own as it comes across new problems; the vision research of Tomaso Poggio and Shimon Ullman, which is intended to shed light on the workings of common human biological visual systems, such as the way people see in stereo, identify and calculate motion and compute the spatial dimensions of objects; and Patrick Winston's painstaking inquiries into how strong a role analogies play in people's reasoning skills.

The Artificial Intelligence Lab has laid a rightful claim to being a seductively exciting research center. Along with major computer figures, academic luminaries from related though separate fields have been attracted by its open-ended research policies. Leading researchers from the neurosciences and psychology, for example, have been lured to its doors to assist computer scientists in unraveling some of the most stubborn details of human intelligence which they will then attempt to transfer, in some form, onto a computer's circuitry.

One of the best known of this group of cross-fertilizers is Whitman Richards, an MIT professor of psychology and human-vision theorist who, during the past decade, switched specialties from traditional psychology to computer science. He is now being touted by many as responsible for pushing computer vision research at MIT into fresh territory totally unanticipated until his ideas arrived.

Richards's academic career is the story of a slow and deliberate psychological researcher. In 1965, he began his initial experiments in human vision techniques. Relying on laborious, time-consuming behavioral studies, he first researched a topic, tested subjects in a random group as well as a control group, graphed the results into statistics, analyzed the numbers, reached conclusions and then retested for secondary validation. Richards spent years combing human sight for clues to its most innate properties. It was time well spent—eventually forming the philosophical backbone of his theories—but the pace was wearying nonetheless.

Finally in 1977, after he learned of the computer vision research then just getting underway in artificial-intelligence centers around the country, and then witnessed it firsthand at the MIT Lab, Richards radically shifted his academic direction. He found in the computer a productive tool that could be used to test his human vision theories and determine their efficacy much more quickly than is the case using traditional psychological testing methods. He also found the computer to be a disciplinary tool. Because it provides relatively immediate results and conclusions, it pushes theorists (who by nature work at less than dizzying speeds) into more fruitful hands-on research in a shorter time.

"The computer is an impartial judge, it will not tolerate halfway work," says Richards. "In order to say you understand vision if you are using a computer as a research tool you must be precise about your approach. It's not enough to say it probably works this way or that way; you must literally take an external image—a scene—direct it into the computer, and show that the computer is able to recover that image in its memory. Then you have proven that you understand at least some part of how the visual process works, because you have made the machine emulate it. The computer enforces that type of rigorousness on your research. Vision is a very complicated information processing system and no conclusions about it should be considered clear or accurate unless they are put to the test. The computer facilitates the testing."

Richards has always felt that visual processes are perhaps the most difficult to unmask. And after following the industrial computer vision research over the past few years, he is strongly convinced that it has done little to describe how handily human sight and knowledge complement each other in the design of our intelligence. A major limitation—that computers can only see unoccluded objects about which they have strong data models—highlights the wide separation between what has been accomplished today and what is ultimately necessary for machines to be able to truly see. To be sure, people rely on strong memory models to identify what they are seeing. But these models are not as exclusively visual as industrial computer vision research would suggest. Rather, human memory models are also stacked with experiential heuristic knowledge, which enables us to identify scenes and prepare to deal with them simultaneously. At best, Richards says, the weakness of today's computer vision processing underlines the fact that an entirely new approach—a more holistic one perhaps—is needed for machine vision perception to lead to widely useful robots.

"Industrial problems are trivial compared to understanding how we see," Richards says. "In real-world human situations, there are actually no possible templates or models that will work across all possible visual situations." The only objective in template-matching computer-vision systems is for the computer to compare raw visual data about an object against a model in its memory. This is the basis of almost all current vision research, including Bolles and Cain's. Disdainfully, most advanced vision researchers point out that template matching is a technique found most commonly in the recognition systems of lower animals. The blowfly, for instance, eats when its receptors match the simple ring structure of a sugar against its model of it. In like fashion, the hungry fledgling gull in its nest responds immediately to the red spot on its parent's beak flying toward it. In the case of these lower animals, their visual systems are programmed to recognize a simple stimulus or pattern that they see as representing something of importance, such as a way to satisfy hunger.

"The red spot on the beak of the gull works as a visual template in the memory of the fledgling gull because from its nest it will almost never encounter other instances of looming red dots—such as traffic lights or red balloons," Richards explains. "In this case a simple template matching strategy works well because of the controlled context. A simple visual question is enough to make reliable assertions about a complex event, namely that a parent has arrived, presumably with food. The situation becomes considerably more complicated, however, for a general-purpose perceptual system like ours that must respond intelligently to a wide range of events in a variety of contexts. We cannot hope to store in our memories attributes or features unique for each event of interest and for each possible contextual situation. It is simply too inefficient a system."

To overcome the apparent flaw in using only templates to model sophisticated human vision on a computer, Richards has developed a unique theory that calls for a computer to quiz itself and its sensors about objects it sees.

Essentially the computer is programmed to ask the same kinds of relevant questions about objects as people would to determine the objects' identities, their place in the scene, what other objects can be expected nearby and so on. The aim is to uncover the innate properties of objects so that the computer has some intelligent direction to use when trying to identify them. For instance, it might ask itself about an object's texture: If it's fine, it's probably an animal; if it's smooth, it is most likely a plant; and if it's rough, consider a mineral.

Interestingly, though Richards is mainly involved with vision, his computer uses the whole range of sensory data —the object's temperature and its acoustic frequency among others—as clues to help it figure out what it is looking at. Richards's approach holds a great deal of promise because it is based on scripts and heuristics; in essence, it attempts to transfer to the computer many of the same human mental skills discovered by other successful artificial-intelligence researchers in different parts of the discipline.

More seriously than whimsically, Richards compares his ideas on vision perception to the game Twenty Questions, where the goal is to identify an object by eliciting the answers to twenty basic questions about it. "When people play Twenty Questions," Richards says, "the first questions usually attempt to identify the general class of the object. Is it an animal, vegetable or mineral? Subsequent questions attempt to determine the size, shape or mass, or the sounds it might make, how it moves or perhaps its functions. The final questions then become very specific and detailed. If we are clever and shrewd in our choices, we rapidly converge to the object. Why can't a perceptual system be designed along similar lines?"

When we look at a scene, we attempt to make it less ambiguous. But in doing so, our goal is not to separate each object from the others in the environment; nor do we turn objects into raw data only to be matched against a memory template, as current vision computers do. Instead, we use the full range of our experiences to go beyond identifying, to decipher the meaning and purpose of objects—to uncover their function in the world. Using the estimable power of parallel processing that our brains are capable of, we determine what an object is while virtually simultaneously organizing a means and plan of interacting with it. Then, seemingly in the same breath, we create a series of expectations that tell us which objects we will probably encounter next. In a block-upon-block fashion, though the blocks can be said to melt into each other even as they are stacked, each move we make to determine what we are looking at helps us in describing what we subsequently see.

"People zero in on a patch or region of an image and make an assertion about what it is in the world and what its world is likely to hold," Richards explains. "Water behaves differently from dirt. Have you ever seen dirt sparkle? Have you ever seen moving waves on dirt? So if we see something that sparkles and has moving waves, we assume it is water. We immediately know the difference between water and dirt not only because of the raw image data we extract from it, but because of its innate characteristics. They are different images in our minds because of the physics behind them. In some sense, our inference proceeds as a result of the questions we ask about what we are seeing. The computer I am developing will similarly ask itself what *it* sees in terms of intrinsic properties and, in this case, say it is in the presence of water not rock.

"Further, if we determine that it's water that we're looking at, then we are probably not going to look for an airplane. Instead, we might look for a fish or a boat or a log. And if we see a blob on the water, it is probably floating so that rules out fish. Now we figure it's a boat or a log, or possibly a resting bird. That is a higher-level inference similar to people's that the computer is able to make from its one determination that it is looking at water."

The key to Richards's theory is the combining of intelligence born of both experience and knowledge with traditional visual information to produce a useful and well-rounded description of a scene. At this point, Richards has not yet attempted a full-blown test of visual Twenty Questions on a computer. However, partial question-and-answer sessions with the machine have led him to believe that his theory is workable if the basic technology required for the computer to retrieve data from the environment is improved.

Therein lie the constraints on his work. For instance, while the question of whether an object scintillates (water), sways (perhaps a plant) or moves laterally (an animal) can be answered by a computer with the most primitive video eyes (provided the background is stationary), the exact shape of an object cannot yet be determined reliably because of such variables as shadows, surface markings, etc. For this limitation, Bolles and Cain's work with using distinct features to identify the complete object may eventually provide a solution. Richards adds that "answering questions such as how many supports or legs are present seems feasible in the near term from the industrial vision advances being developed today. But today the computer is unable to make a sufficiently powerful sketch of an object to permit these questions to be answered."

Similarly, in the audio realm, sensors that measure acoustic frequencies and sound-intensity changes have been available for many years. (As a general statement, if the computer "hears" broad-band sounds, they are likely coming from plants, minerals or very large animals; narrow-band sounds are made by smaller creatures.) Pinpointing the object emitting the sound in a complicated environment, however, is not so easily achieved.

"As long as the environment does not have more than one or two competing sources, the source direction of the sound can be found using either signal onset times or intensity difference or both," Richards explains. "Additional work needs to be done in these areas, however, because in most cases there is more than one competing sound being made at the same time. Source direction is a critical characteristic to be discerned, especially if it is desired to determine details about the physical properties of the source—is it metallic, wood or rustling leaves—or the nature of the animal sounds.

"It is still uncertain the extent to which the technology of the near future can give reliable answers to all the questions I would like the computer to pose to itself. Those that concern shape appear particularly difficult, whereas those that address the properties, composition or size of the object seem more tractable. Improving the visual and acoustic capabilities that a computer has for seeing its environment is a great challenge."

To illustrate Richards's theories, here is a hypothetical example of the computer's internal self-questioning and thought processes as it attempts to identify an object. The only fact given the computer is that the habitat is a temperate environment with green rolling hills.

Question 1: Is it moving?
Answer: It translates.

Note: The word translation, as it is used here, means the movement of an object from one place to another. Translation, therefore, is usually the property of animals, and not vegetables or minerals. The computer now would assume it is looking at an animal of some type.

Question 2: How many supports does it have?
Answer: Four.

Note: This would confirm the presence of an animal; a plant would probably have one support and a mineral none.

*According to Richards, to estimate the number of supports first the ground plane must be determined; secondly, the support itself must be recognized; and finally, an object has to be identified as being supported although its chassis may have a different color or texture from its base. Additionally, shrubs may ap-*

*pear to have many supports. This is one question that is still very difficult to rely on.*

Question 3: What acoustic frequencies are emitted?
Answer: Low-frequency, broad-band sounds.
Note: This would lead the computer to conclude it is not a small animal. It may be an elephant or a cow.
*Richards adds that the answer to this question would be far more useful if the computer could extract the physical properties of the source, such as its acoustic color: Is it metallic, wood striking wood, a footfall, smooth or roaring like a brook or a lion. However, there are no sensors yet able to determine such physical properties.*

Question 4: What is the acoustic source?
Answer: From one point, rather than extended.
Note: Again this confirms an animal or an isolated object.

Question 5: What is its axis?
Answer: Horizontal.
Note: The computer would still think it is some kind of large animal.

Question 6: What is its color?
Answer: Blue.

Note: The computer would "know" that a blue animal is unlikely. It retains this new bit of data as an anomaly to its previously known information. It searches its memory for something like an animal that may be blue.
*Richards points out that it is fairly easy to determine an object's color. Spectral video machines in common use for assessing food quality, printing inks or photographic reproductions can be used for this task.*

Question 7: What is its hardness?
Answer: Hard rather than soft or elastic (animal) or crunchy or crisp (plant).

Note: Though the fact that it is hard would generally lead the computer to conclude it is a mineral, all other previously gained information dictates against this assumption. The computer has now rejected animal, plant or mineral, but by rummaging through the data in its memory it now leans to a car as the possible object it is looking at.
*Richards notes that assessing hardness is a trivial task considering the constant development of new and better devices able to detect the hardness or softness of distant objects.*

Question 8: What is it rate of leg motion?
Answer: Zero.

Note: The object, thus, has no legs, but it has four supports and moves. The computer guesses that the supports are wheels and the object is a blue car.

The excitement generated in the artificial-intelligence community by Richards's approach to vision perception is similar to that which hailed Roger Schank's work in natural language and James Reggia's frame approach to knowledge in expert systems. Playing a visual version of Twenty Questions provides a heuristic and holistic foundation for emulating human vision on a computer. Having been devised by a psychological researcher, it is an attempt to be faithful on its own scale to neurological processes in people.

There are, of course, windows of technological vulnerability in Richards's computer program. For instance, the computer can easily be badly misled by Question 1 or Question 2. If the answer to "motion" is "none" it would be difficult to infer that the object is an animal; but it may be a stationary animal, lying down. Further, a prone animal will appear to have no legs and will probably emit no sounds. The computer's hypotheses will be thrown way off the mark. As yet there is no solution to this built-in error potential. The hope, though, is that improved vision and other sensory devices will drive up the importance and reliability of other questions in the examination session and, in so doing, alert the computer that it may be being deceived by an object in a less-than-usual posture.

A simple Twenty Questions game is meant to be a springboard for a much richer interpretation of the scene by the computer. It is a baseline, as Richards puts it, from which more detailed explorations of the observed data can be made. These explorations can take many directions. The most obvious, Richards says, are secondary question-and-answer sessions that zoom in on the identified object and examine its parts, like the fruit on a tree or the face of a man.

"Consider that the first pass-through of the twenty questions yielded the object Animal [catlike]," Richards explains. "The next step would be to obtain more information about the actions, posture or behavior of the animal. Although we might already know it is moving toward the tree, is it making friendly or aggressive noises, is its tail stiff or its teeth bared and its claws extended?"

Once an object is identified as an animal, then many components of the scene that may have been ambiguous at first glance are now more readily understood. This mimics the human visual attribute of building upon blocks of inferred knowledge to identify higher and higher levels of knowledge about a scene. For instance, bared teeth might look like rows of rocks at first, but if the object is deemed to be an animal, closer examination of it would reject the possibility that it is seeing rows of rocks lined up on the animal's face; instead, the computer would conclude that the white swatch is the animal's teeth bandied in an aggressive display.

Of the hundreds of artificial-intelligence researchers examining vision, Richards is one of the most original. He is clearly raising the stakes on what it is possible to teach computers to see. Over the next five years, his theories—or variations of them created by other researchers—will likely lead to a much higher plane of achievement in this area than has been attained up to now. The sighted robot, ready to investigate deep water channels or clean up miles of spilled toxics, will not be an unusual fixture in working human society, by most accounts, in the 1990s.

## Chapter 7

# THOSE WHO PAY THE FREIGHT

Bob Kahn is an energetic government bureaucrat whose soft-spoken manner belies the fact that he is known as a brash decision maker responsible for doling out close to $100 million a year for basic and applied research in artificial intelligence. In less-staid circles of artificial intelligence, he is known as the Godfather—the one man who ultimately decides the fate of almost every artificial-intelligence project conceived. It's a simple fact: Without the federal government—specifically, without Bob Kahn's tiny agency located in the catacombs of the labyrinthine Defense Department—academic artificial-intelligence research in this country would be fighting over limited private endowment funds instead of basking in the relatively undemanding support from Washington.

The agency is called the Defense Advanced Research

Projects Agency or, more commonly, DARPA; Kahn is the director of its Information Processing Techniques Office. DARPA came into being in 1958 as part of the furor touched off by the Soviet's launching of the Sputnik satellite a year earlier. Policymakers felt then that for the United States to retain its worldwide superiority in technology, a scientific watchdog agency needed to be established. The purpose of this agency would be to roam the corridors of academia and, to a lesser degree, corporate America, searching for esoteric but potentially useful research to ply with government support. In fulfilling this role, DARPA does no research on its own; instead, it finances, advises, holds hands and strokes workers in a wide variety of high-tech disciplines as they pursue their aims.

The impact that DARPA-funded research has had is somewhat difficult to measure. Because of the secrecy involved in the development of military-related technology, a widespread awareness of much of this research trickles down into the industrial and commercial sectors only *after* the DARPA label has essentially been removed. But a close look reveals that DARPA has sponsored some of the most important technological developments extant. Two esoteric, but crucial, agency-sponsored research projects immediately come to mind: virtual computer memory, which extends the basic useable memory of a computer by as much as twentyfold with simple programming tricks (IBM was the first commercial company to rely on this breakthrough to open up the power gates of its computers—now most computer firms are using it); and packet switching, which greatly speeds up the processing of digital and verbal data over phone and cable lines. (AT&T embraced this technology initially and it is now a ubiquitous component of telecommunications designs.) American business today would come to a relative standstill without either of these advances, though they may seem less than household items. DARPA has played the role of silent partner in their development. And the same is true with regard to artificial-intelligence research. Few major advances in this discipline over the past twenty-five years would have occurred without DARPA's financial support, though it is has perhaps taken a backseat in terms of publicity.

Since its inception, DARPA has performed its job with an efficiency and aplomb rare among Washington's bureaucracies. Like a dwarf amidst giant DOD departments, this diminutive agency (by Pentagon standards) has been mostly immune to and isolated from the ups and downs of the defense budget, the verbal tumults over military contractors who have bilked taxpayers for billions of dollars, and the cries that defense dollars, in general, bring in far less than they promise.

"Perhaps we remain above the fray because, at the heart, we are an agency of very basic research, not applied technologies, so it is far more difficult to quantify our achievements," says Kahn. "It's probably tougher to measure how well we are doing our job for that reason." Kahn adds that despite DARPA's unique position in the Defense Department, it does not consider itself a maverick agency. "We are keenly aware that we are an integral part of the Defense Department," Kahn says. "All the work that we support is intended for some military purpose ultimately. It is important to note, though, that how the military uses the research is solely up to other decision makers at other parts of the Pentagon. We are not responsible for implementing the applications that come out of our research. We just provide the conclusions and the results."

Kahn has been at DARPA since 1972, when he left a professorship in electronic engineering at MIT to pursue government administration. Since arriving at DARPA, Kahn has been enamored of artificial intelligence and how it could powerfully influence computer development over the next decades. Though artificial intelligence has not wanted for DARPA funding over the past ten years, Kahn and a group of colleagues at the agency recently decided that a cohesive program was needed in this age of great technological expectations to push the discipline into much higher gear. Consequently, in 1983 they put forth a wildly ambitious $600 million, five-year research program into artificial intelligence and microelectronics that promises to place the United States on the cutting edge of the leading breakthroughs in defense and commercial high technology.

This latest DARPA artificial-intelligence effort is the culmination of nearly thirty years of collaboration between the discipline and the Defense Department. The history of DARPA's relationship to artificial intelligence is interesting and instructive. It provides a case study of a government agency that has been less than unimpeachable in its funding decisions, but has managed to gracefully skirt the shifting tides of Congressional opinion and ride the waves of technological advance. Though it is uncharacteristic for a Pentagon department, DARPA has, in its artificial-intelligence effort, been able to shift gears and orchestrate well-chosen new policy directions with little obvious effort.

DARPA's involvement with artificial intelligence began

right after the pivotal 1956 Dartmouth conference when the discipline went public. The main achievement of the conference was setting the wheels in motion for funding—and DARPA was the vehicle that would pay the freight.

"DARPA single-handedly created artificial intelligence with its funding power," says Steve Andriole, the expert-system builder now working on a project for the Army. Andriole, from 1976 through 1979, was director for the now-defunct Office of Cybernetic Technology at DARPA. During that time he was responsible for financing the work of Yale's Roger Schank and Carnegie-Mellon's Jaime Carbonell among many others. "DARPA was attracted to artificial intelligence because DARPA's mission was, and continues to be, to fund high-risk, but potentially high-payoff research. The goals of artificial intelligence as they were described from the beginning—to create machines that think—dovetailed perfectly with the agency's commitment."

The efficacy of the artificial-intelligence projects it funded originally mattered little to DARPA in the earliest stages of the relationship. The agency was less than rigorous in its investigation of the proposed artificial-intelligence research. Taken by the hyperbolic promises of the first wave of artificial intelligence, DARPA money was freely given to many of the projects that merely simulated and mimicked human intelligence.

A classic manifestation of this loose funding policy was the rash of so-called translation programs that DARPA financed in the late 1960s. If a machine could translate documents with the fluency of human decoding experts—and hopefully faster—planners reasoned that the nation's defenses would be bolstered significantly. As this was before Schank and his breakthrough work in linguistics and natural languages, these translation programs did not use contextual analysis of phrases or, certainly, scripts, but strictly relied on so-called syntactical decoding. Word for word, with no regard for the subtleties of the languages, cultures and grammar involved, the computers attempted to decode what was being said or written. The results could be farcical, if millions of dollars had not gone into producing them. One of these computers came up with the now-infamous translation of the phrase, input in Russian, "The spirit is willing, but the flesh is weak." The computer concluded in English: "The vodka is good, but the meat is rotten."

According to former DARPA insiders, one major reason exists for DARPA's ill-fated relationship with less-than-worthy artificial-intelligence projects from the 1950s through the early 1970s: The artificial-intelligence community, by default, drove the funding mechanism at the agency. Academic leaders of the field decided which approaches to artificial intelligence deserved grants and which should be rejected, and all of the prime movers in artificial intelligence were seduced by the potential of brute-force programming, of which the translation systems were a prime example. The relationship between DARPA and these academics could actually have started in no other way. There were simply few people in the country who understood artificial intelligence in its early days—and none of these people were in government.

Thus, purely because of ignorance, congressional overseers failed to give close scrutiny to the quality of artificial-intelligence projects DARPA chose to fund. Moreover, the agency itself was unable to create a set of criteria to use as a guide to how the money should be dispensed.

Increasingly, though, as the 1970s began, DARPA officials grew restless, concerned that the academic proposals they were endorsing were not proving out. Clearly, very little machine intelligence was emerging at all from the millions of dollars being poured into the discipline. DARPA officials were beginning to correctly conclude that artificial intelligence—at least in the way that the leaders of its first wave defined and ballyhooed it—was less than deserving of continued high-priced funding. Artificial intelligence could have been severely hurt by this realization at the agency but, instead, a completely unexpected Pentagon policy move occurred that actually improved the funding climate for the discipline. Though the more traditional channels of the Defense Department had largely ignored artificial intelligence up until then, suddenly under widespread pressure to improve its military capabilities, primarily because of failures in the Vietnamese War, the DOD began to look to artificial intelligence as a means of upgrading and modernizing what was perceived as the nation's weakened defense posture.

As Stephen Andriole remembers those years: "Congressional Armed Services Committees in the House and Senate in the period around 1973 and on began to badger the Defense Department about what it intends to do to improve its ability to fight a full-scale war, one waged possibly on many fronts. So those testifying for the services countered with, 'Well, we've got this technology called artificial intelligence that DARPA has been funding for many years which is building machines that can actually think. By 1985, so we've been promised, this technology will be realized so greatly that we can safely expect to have weapons that are literally smart.' And this got Congress interested, because if it were to believe the Defense Department, it would in effect be mortgaging the future of weapons development on the success of artificial intelligence.

"So when the time came for the hearings on DARPA funding, the leaders at DARPA were told by Congress, 'What are you doing in artificial intelligence? We're hearing from a lot of guys at the Pentagon that you're making a lot of progress.' And the committee wanted to know who was getting the financing, what were the results of the various experiments, what are the eventual applications of the research; in other words, what are we getting for our investments and will it all be useful? The representatives wanted concrete answers. They wouldn't be happy anymore, for example, with a response like, 'We're improving the knowledge base of artificial intelligence.' "

Faced with this increased Congressional scrutiny—and committee staffs in the House and Senate were beefed up with investigators fluent in all areas of high technology during this period—DARPA officials set up an internal timetable designed to make artificial intelligence more of a useful science and less of an esoteric and, up to then, useless one. To this end, a massive hiring drive was begun. People like Bob Kahn and Stephen Andriole, who were well versed in computers and microelectronics, were brought into the agency. And the former DARPA employment policy of hiring government administrators who were mostly non-technologists was shelved.

The new employees' task was twofold: examine closely all funded projects for their potential usefulness; and work on getting these projects into the applied technology sector more rapidly than before. DARPA's new direction was a stroke of genius and an excellent example of how easily the agency is able to respond to criticism and scrutiny from its regulators in Washington.

To fulfill the first portion of their self-imposed mandate, DARPA officials let it be known that in the future they would be deciding which projects deserved money; the individual, high-tech communities themselves would not drive the funding process anymore. What this meant was expanded financial coverage for the second wave of artificial-intelligence research, work involved with machine knowledge and learning through the use of heuristics, scripts, contextual-language understanding, knowledge-based vision perception and other processes based directly on human mental skills. Over $20 million a year is now taken from the public coffers for this type of work, but it receives far stricter Congressional scrutiny than ever before. The DARPA program is now considered to be on a correct path.

The second portion of the mandate—to speed up the timetable for applying basic research to the technological sector—was fulfilled in a dramatic way in 1983 with the announcement of the Strategic Computing Program, a plan to take the previous ten years of artificial-intelligence research and translate it directly into useable military applications. "This program is a direct result of our involvement with artificial intelligence over the years," Bob Kahn says. "But the important difference is that we chose the technologies that we knew would be successful in an applied setting. We worked far more closely with the Defense Department when we set up the Strategic Computing Program than perhaps we ever have before. We asked the folks at the Pentagon to give us a wish list of the types of applications they would like to put artificial intelligence in and from that list we chose those projects that seemed workable from our understanding of the discipline."

What resulted was a plan to build three separate devices incorporating to a large degree all of the most successful artificial-intelligence findings to date; specifically, vision perception, expert systems and natural languages. These devices included a battle-management expert system that, while interacting with military strategists with both speech and natural language, would be able to display detailed pictures of battle zones, forecast enemy intent and generate potential courses of action; a pilot's associate that, again using natural language and advances in computer speech techniques, would serve as a personal aid trained by the individual pilot to perform those tasks that he finds most taxing in a tense wartime situation (for instance, it might be instructed to automatically reconfigure the sensitivity of the aircraft's controls to the preferences of the pilot if a wing is damaged during combat); and a driverless robotic land vehicle that would plan and navigate a cross-country route and report back its findings and interpretations of what it saw during its travels.

The Strategic Computing Program met with favorable notices in the artificial-intelligence community and in Washington almost from the moment it was announced. The Pentagon sees it as a way of integrating the most advanced technology available into the mainstream of its military plans for the future. Congressional leaders call it a justification for all the money spent on basic research through DARPA over the years. This chorus of approval has led to $50 million in funding for the program in fiscal year 1984 and nearly $100 million in fiscal year 1985. Also, it assures that the annual $20 million or so in artificial-intelligence basic research funds will not be tampered with. Importantly, fitting with the emphasis in this program on applied and not theoretical research, for the first time in DARPA's history with artificial intelligence, much of the funding for the Strategic Computing Program will be disbursed to corporate America, to firms like IBM, Texas Instruments, SRI and the like, rather than to academia.

For the military, this new program has not been proposed a moment too soon. Many proposals for so-called Star Wars defense plans have been put forth by non-technologists—the President, Secretary of Defense, general military strategists—and those working in high-tech defense industries have been hard pressed to keep pace with the fantasies implicit in the laymen's promises. Out of ignorance, the non-technologists have generated a great deal of dismay among military technologists by confusing present-day, dumb computer technology with artificial intelligence, which would fit well with the Star Wars concept. Today's computers are being touted as far more capable of performing intelligently in high-tech warfare than they actually are. In fact, attempts to wage actual or mock battles using the current crop of dumb computer hardware and software have been mostly disastrous.

"The ability of present-day computers to assist in complex combat activities is limited, because their computational capability cannot handle highly complex unstructured environments," DARPA officials wrote in a recent report on Defense Department high-tech efforts. "In addition, their ability to relate to humans . . . is so cognitively inefficient that it is doubtful the person could receive, interpret and act on the information in time even if it were available in the machine."

They point to an actual example that occurred in a conflict not long ago. The event involved a sophisticated type of radar specifically designed to track aircraft without being confused by decoys. But in this particular case the enemy forces, understanding the limits of the radar the United States was using, approached by air in groups of four planes that rapidly branched out in four different directions. The computerized radar reacted by jittering like a directionless loon from one craft to the other until it lost track of all four. The solution, of course, was to rewrite the software, but there was no way for the forces in the field to attempt this. It had to be accomplished at headquarters and then flown out into the field.

"Even with a crash program," the DARPA officials note, "it took several days to eliminate the radar's inflexibility when responding to a simple change of tactics that had not been anticipated by the radar designers."

Those in or close to the Pentagon are able to speak for long hours about the numerous snafus caused by today's computers put into the battle environment; many disdain, from a military perspective, the power of current computer technology. Though they agree that computers can lead to a scenario of warfare unlike any other ever devised, they privately say that only if highly cognitive machines, like the robotic land vehicle in the Strategic Computing Program, are perfected will computerized defense truly be a useful reality.

The robotic land vehicle is often pointed to as the perfect example of how machine intelligence will become a part of military strategy. This driverless vehicle is supposed to travel at speeds of up to sixty kilometers per hour (37 mph) over any type of terrain and be used for such missions as deep-penetration reconnaissance, resupply of troops at the front, sensitive munitions handling and weapons delivery. Like each of the devices in the Strategic Computing Program, this vehicle is an ambitious undertaking, one that stretches the limits of artificial-intelligence research by an unfathomable degree.

Its vision perception system will have to be a far cry from what is available today, which can recognize little more than basic geometric shapes in uncomplicated environments. "The vehicle's vision system will recognize roads and their boundaries," Bob Kahn says, "and select, locate and size up obstacles in the roadway. Additionally, it will have to detect, locate and identify manmade and natural landmarks and produce maps of the local environment while moving at its highest speeds."

Kahn adds that the computing power needed for this vision system will be as high as 100 billion instructions per second, in traditional computer terms (as compared to the 40 million instructions per second computers are capable of today). DARPA officials are banking on significant improvements in microelectronics and chip development—specifically the design of very-high-speed semiconductors, capable of parallel processing—to accomplish this rapid rise in computational horsepower.

The expert system on board the vehicle will be equally remarkable. As Kahn describes it: "It will plan its own routes using digital terrain and environmental data, devise strategies for avoiding unanticipated obstacles, estimate the vehicle's position, generate moment-to-moment steering and speed commands, monitor onboard conditions and finally generate battle information from what it has seen." An expert system for the robotic land vehicle will require the ability to maintain 6500 rules, thinking at the pace of 7000 rules per second. Even the most far-reaching expert system today only contains 2000 rules and at its fastest speed can read a mere 100 rules per second.

Add to all of this the requirements that the vehicle's computer will have to hold a memory of 10 gigabytes, be about six cubic feet in volume, weigh less than 500 pounds and consume only a kilowatt of electricity. No current computer comes close to any of these specifications.

Though it all sounds almost too ambitious to be possible, Kahn and his colleagues feel that by using "the nation's well-developed technological infrastructure," as he describes it, the Strategic Computing Program will easily be achieved before the end of the decade. "We may find out in the end that the vehicle will never be able to tell the difference between a bumblebee and a brick wall, to be hyperbolic," Kahn says. "But that one idiosyncracy will be its only one. And we'll correct it before too many years."

Many close to DARPA and the Strategic Computing effort are less sanguine about its chances to leapfrog today's available technology so easily. One researcher at a corporate lab who is involved in developing the visual portion of the autonomous land vehicle has examined the time-line closely and finds it reasonable in the short term, but in the end far too optimistic.

"The first two or three years, they plan to demonstrate the vehicle on paved roads with no cars, animals or other obstacles," the researcher explains. "That is doable. There is a very strong visual model for the computer to work with. It knows it's on a road, its data base tells it what the terrain is like, and how the road travels, and the road's boundaries or edges are well marked. By the third year, they are talking about allowing the computer to locate obstacles on the road. This will need a range-finding vision device that finds big boxes placed in the way, not six inch widgets. Again this is very possible because it will be very limited and with nothing unexpected placed as an obstacle.

"Now over the next few years they are planning on the next dimension: going off road. They're first talking about going slowly, perhaps walking speed. Initially it will be an unpaved road on a generally open terrain like a desert with no big objects protruding. That too is possible. It is an uncomplicated visual model with nothing unusual darting out at the computer.

"But when you get into the next step—thickly packed forests with stumps of various sizes and placements—you have a problem. That is simply implausible considering what we are able to do in vision today. DARPA is clearly hoping that over the next four or five years, this more difficult technology will be worked out in the basic-research arena so it can be applied to its autonomous vehicle when they are ready for it."

Nevertheless, despite the misgivings of some, it is hard to dismiss DARPA's predictions out of hand as public-relations hype. Considering the agency's quiet record of successes in high technology, the Strategic Computing Program may be seen as the most purposeful and mature step ever taken to move artificial intelligence fully into the real-world applications arena, where it will trickle down eventually from the military to more commercial uses.

But DARPA's role as patron to the artificial-intelligence community has led to an interesting schism among researchers in the field. A growing number of younger workers feel uncomfortable with, as one put it, "going to bed with the military each day." They, instead, support the creation of a national science or industrial agency to monitor and support the development of high-technological advances and ensure that they are used for the commonweal. This agency would be similar to the well-publicized Japanese Ministry of International Trade and Industry (MITI), which is challenging the U. S. for supremacy in most computer design research, including superchip development and artificial intelligence. Interestingly, despite the raft of government-support programs hatched each year, legislation has never even been introduced that would take responsibility for high technology away from DARPA.

"What frightens me is the military aspect of all of this," says Edward Hoevy at Yale. "The vision system on the Pershing missile came from primitive research in artificial intelligence. The latest work in surreptitious phone conversation monitoring that the Defense Department is working on also came out of portions of artificial-intelligence research. This is a frightening thing to me who would like to be proud of the fact that I am an artificial-intelligence researcher."

Hoevy recalls a 1983 conference on artificial intelligence in West Germany, during which a European missile company put on a demonstration of their view of the "smart wars" of the future. Hundreds of Germans marched in the streets around the conference hall protesting the presence of the artificial-intelligence conclave and its military-industrial partners. Inside, this led to a discussion among the fifteen hundred researchers present about artificial intelligence and the correctness of its not-so-subtle ties to the defense establishment.

"I—and those many who agree with me—were encouraged by the prospects of this discussion," Hoevy says. "We thought that finally there would be a cogent analysis of our position on this matter. But this was not to be. The leaders in the artificial-intelligence field dominated the microphone with their pro-DARPA rhetoric, inhibiting any chance for those opposing their position to even speak. Finally, many of us walked out in disgust.

"We have a responsibility, since we're creating something that has perhaps the greatest potential societal impact since the atomic bomb, to address how it should be properly controlled. This might sound naive, but if we are stuck with DARPA there should be a panel of societal experts that have to be consulted before any use is made of an intelligent computer. Voluntarily, like sheep, we are pushing ourselves down a very bad path."

Almost to a person, however, the leading figures in artificial intelligence, those holding the highest academic posts in the field, are supportive of DARPA. Of course, the methods of the mutual admiration society are at work here. DARPA has been artificial intelligence's chief backer and has turned what could have been lean years financially into excellent ones. And with the Strategic Computing Program just getting under way, very few charged with keeping university budgets fat would quarrel with the defense agency at this point.

Edward Feigenbaum of Stanford describes DARPA as an agency that understands the concept of spending "relevant sums of money" when supporting basic research. "Even if you call yourself a theorist, as an artificial-intelligence researcher you do experimenting almost all the time," says Feigenbaum. "You build programs, test them, rebuild them and so on. That takes time and it's expensive. DARPA understands that and DARPA provides relevant amounts of money to that end. The National Science Foundation is not of the tradition of supplying relevant sums of money. The NSF takes a given amount of money and spreads it as thinly as possible to cover as many scientists as possible, because it sees itself basically as the supporting arm for all scientists and their graduate students. They don't care if only a few good ideas reach fruition as long as many scientists have been kept fed. DARPA, on the other hand, looks at their support on a per project basis. If you deserve support, it will give it to you and in the right amounts."

Roger Schank, the Yale don, agrees with Feigenbaum, but lives with the paradox of viewing most of the military federal agencies as political adversaries while at the same time recognizing that the Defense Department is the glad hand that keeps his university department and his personal theories in business. "Those of us who would call ourselves political radicals in the 60s and 70s found ourselves in the peculiar situation of loving the Defense Department and hating the FBI and CIA, though they were all involved in the same types of so-called anti-counterculture activities," says Schank. "I think the Defense Department is the most enlightened funding agency there ever was in this country. The record is clear: It is pouring millions and millions of dollars into a purely speculative technology. And I'm not sure with any bad purpose in mind. Whatever you feel about the government, it's not true at DARPA."

Schank recognizes that he is waging an internal conflict between his political views and his efforts to keep his chosen discipline alive and, indeed, to keep bread on his table. But he dismisses this conflict with one concise statement that, he says, overrides all other thoughts on the subject. "If the Defense Department pulls out of artificial intelligence," he says, "there will be no artificial intelligence."

Schank's point is an oft-heard one from those academics who have relied on DARPA for so many years. However, the agency's dominant role as the funding arm for artificial-intelligence research projects may be not as solid as it has been. Though the amounts of money involved, even in the aggregate, are small compared to DARPA's support, during the past few years, many major corporations have begun to pour millions of dollars annually into researching the viability and usefulness of smart machines. The roster of companies staking a claim to this territory reads like the guest list at a party honoring the most successful technological innovators of this century: International Business Machines, Texas Instruments, Hewlett-Packard, Martin

Marietta, American Telephone and Telegraph, Schlumberger, General Motors and Xerox, to name a few.

Each of these companies, in proprietary, closely guarded research centers, is manipulating and recasting some of the most fundamental artificial-intelligence concepts to emerge from academia, hoping to use the technology as a key element in the evolution of its corporate future. Some intend to design hardware and software with artificial intelligence to improve their own design and manufacturing facilities; others plan to sell products using artificial intelligence to consumers. But whichever approach is being taken there is a persistent sense generated by these companies that a high-tech corporation is committing financial suicide if it doesn't begin to get involved in building intelligent computers.

What makes this list of firms especially impressive and noteworthy is the presence of the two largest companies in the world, AT&T and IBM. Indeed, AT&T and IBM are, by most accounts, the strongest supporters of artificial intelligence in corporate America. Though hard figures are difficult to confirm, those close to the two companies say privately that each firm is spending more than $2 million annually on research into advanced computers—both the so-called superchip technology and smart machines. Moreover, that figure is expected to rise significantly over the coming decade as IBM and AT&T compete head-on in the high-tech marketplace, as a result of the phone company's divestiture.

Interestingly, the way these two firms approach artificial-intelligence research could not be more different. In general, over the years, AT&T as a research agency has had few financial worries. It has been able to adopt a stance approaching that of a life-long graduate student supported by never-ending and ample parental funds. Because of its long-time monopoly status, it grew used to the luxury of playing the role of the aloof theorist and plodding gadget maker. AT&T never had to rush to turn laboratory concepts into full-fledged products because it faced no competitors waiting to steal its thunder.

So it is even now with its artificial-intelligence research. Despite its new status as a contender in a hotly competitive field, very few practical and overly demanding questions are asked of the artificial-intelligence workers at AT&T; they are never compelled to justify their hours or make predictions as to how close they are to completion or to which commercial applications their work would best lend itself. The atmosphere among researchers at AT&T is relaxed and free of the produce-or-perish pressure that is common in many corporate think tanks.

IBM provides a direct contrast. As history's most tenaciously successful high-tech company in a nonmonopolistic environment, IBM has acquired an imperious tone that pervades its actions and rubs off on even its basic researchers. Artificial-intelligence workers at IBM are not so much trampled by imposed timetables from above; rather they are driven by the carefully promulgated idea that they must be loyal supporters of the team if the company is to retain its vitality. Thus the researchers feel obliged to offer tangible results quickly, not out of a fear for their jobs, but more out of the realization that their ability to produce at a quick pace will mean continued high-tech supremacy for the corporation. As one researcher put it bluntly: "There is an orchestrated undercurrent here that tells us that our work serves to feed the giant and make it stronger."

In terms of overall research and development, IBM is the hands-down leader in the corporate world. Its research arm has twenty-six locations in twelve states and overseas sites in Japan, France, Britain, Germany and Switzerland. It employs 370,000 researchers and support staff and enjoys a whopping annual budget of $2.5 billion, 10 percent of which is for pure basic research.

AT&T's research subsidiary, Bell Labs, sports figures only slightly less impressive. Bell Labs, which has been providing the parent company with new communications technology since 1925, has thirteen outposts in six states and employs 19,000. Despite smaller numbers in those categories, its annual budget is a massive $1.9 billion, again with 10 percent targeted for basic research.

The central home of Bell Labs is located in Murray Hill, New Jersey, a soft-sloping surburban region in the center of the state. The town seems to epitomize in its sleepiness and quiet unobtrusiveness the phrase *bedroom community.*

Bell Labs is in sharp contrast to its environs. The muted ranch houses and split-level frames on symmetrical lots that line most roads in Murray Hill are overshadowed by AT&T's two-hundred-acre research site with its winding bicycle and jogging paths and huge central building—a dense brick and glass structure with tentaclelike wings that connect the disparate quads on the Bell Labs campus. The building has the eerie, sullen appearance of a lunar module having just landed in an unassuming town.

Inside, Bell Labs is a swarming hive of activity. The one

tangible product produced there, information, is shared freely. In an age when privacy in business is guarded religiously, AT&T, out of an old habit formed when it had no competition, still keeps little of what it is working on secret —at least in the basic research stage. Visitors arrive each day from foreign scientific delegations, academic research mills, U.S. technological agencies such as NASA and the CIA, independent telephone companies and the high-tech contractor community; Bell researchers parade their latest insights like newly discovered gems before an appreciative audience.

The artificial-intelligence work at Bell Labs has few limits in terms of breadth. Every important avenue of research in the discipline is under investigation, from natural-language work, including computer speech synthesis, to vision perception to automation of the expert-system designing process. Most of the researchers are serious and typically quiet scientists, but one of them is decidedly not of this mold.

Mitch Marcus is a loquacious artificial-intelligence worker who is basking in a growing and estimable reputation as a natural-language researcher. He is one of those excited, confident scientists who is almost rhapsodic when describing the nature of his work down to its most intimate details. He confesses that he enjoys grappling with peers who disagree with his sometimes unorthodox theories. It is a small conceit; he is known as one of artificial intelligence's most able debaters, who in the end can make colleagues question their own conclusions. Ensconced in a tiny eight-foot-square office in sprawling Bell Labs, with only a computer terminal to communicate with much of the day, he seems to revel in any spotlight that comes along.

After an academic career that spanned degrees in linguistics and computer science at Harvard and a PhD from the Artificial Intelligence Lab at MIT, Marcus came to Bell Labs in 1979 with a hunch about language that he wanted to test out on computers. Like Roger Schank at Yale, he realized that language is a key to unlock deep mysteries of intelligence. But unlike Schank he did not think that only scripts, which contain general world knowledge, should be used to teach computers language understanding. Certain specific syntactical and grammatical information must coexist with scripts in the computer's memory, he felt.

"Schank and I have back-to-back papers in a recent book where I argue that his view is wrong in this one aspect," Marcus says. "Otherwise his views are quite remarkable. But he believes that there isn't an iota of intelligence about syntax and grammar in the part of our heads that understands language. Well, I think that the evidence is in fact overwhelming that every time we hear a sentence the first thing we do is automatically analyze the grammar of the sentence; that is the initial step to computing its meaning. Schank thinks we go straight to breaking the sentence up into knowledge compartments, not grammatical elements. I disagree."

Marcus could have continued his natural-language research at MIT, but he opted to move to Bell Labs because in the academic world he would have constantly had to rejustify his work for DARPA or other grant agencies. Bell offered him an open-ended invitation, essentially, to delve into his theories with little fear that the rug would be pulled out from under him if he did not produce in a short time.

"One of the main reasons I came here is because I decided I would have more freedom at Bell Labs than I would in academia," Marcus says. "I am much less directed than I would be as a university researcher getting my money from DARPA and having to write a paper at the end of each quarter describing how my work is going to be useful soon. Ultimately, yes, the research at Bell is intended to be used in some application, and in that sense there are very few poets at Bell, but mind you only in that sense. No one inside here has ever pressed me to describe what application my work will ultimately be put to."

That is not to say that there is no quality-control mechanism at AT&T's research arm. In fact, there is a very rigorous one. It's simply that, just as AT&T lacks the type of fear usually engendered by competition, the review process has been worn down over time. As the researcher-review mechanism is formally constituted at Bell, each researcher meets with his department head once a year and describes in detail either orally or on paper what he's accomplished during the past twelve months and what his projections are for the next twelve months. The department head passes this report on to his supervisor and incrementally it moves up the ladder, through Bell Labs and then on to the parent company. Additionally, supervisors from AT&T and Bell Labs, from time to time, will ask a certain group, perhaps the robotics researchers, to demonstrate its theories and conclusions in full-day seminars. Marcus has never really seen the overseeing mechanism in operation, however. "My manager always knows what I'm doing," he says, "because he's one of the people I talk to a lot. There's no necessity for me to give him a full-fledged report each year."

The focus of Marcus's natural-language theories is on something called a semantics box. Essentially, this box directly precedes, in the computer's memory, the compartment that contains the machine's world knowledge or scripts. The semantics box is programmed with basic grammatical and syntactical rules. An incoming sentence would first have to pass through the semantics box, where it is broken apart and identified in terms of its prime grammatical elements and their semantic relations, before it could proceed to the scripts area, where it will be attached to relevant world information.

As an example, Marcus points to a sentence that Schank himself has used to show the utter ambiguity of language: "John gave Mary a beating." There are many different senses of the verb "to give"; this sentence contains a less-than-primary, idiomatic use of the verb. Translated into a form that makes the meaning clearer to the computer, the sentence would read, "John beat up Mary." Making such a translation is the work of Marcus's semantics box.

If the sentence was not translated first, Marcus argues, and was thrown into Schank's scripts system in its original form, the computer would spend much more time searching through the system for the appropriate script. First, it would attempt to attach the sentence to its "gift giving" script and, after passing it through a few times for comprehension, find it totally irrelevant. Then, it would see if the sentence fits into its "bath, haircut, shower" script and again find it a poor match and incomprehensible. Finally, and much later, it would settle on the correct script to use in this case. Marcus says his system simplifies and economizes the search time to a significant degree by merely applying some of the same basics of grammar and semantics any child would be taught in primary education.

"The general metaphor for my theory," Marcus explains, "is in the idea of a stream that you want to cross. One way to cross the stream is to take a hurdling broad jump, as Schank proposes by sending the sentence directly to the scripts part of the program, and perhaps fall flat on your face in the process. The other way is to find a few stones in the middle of the stream and jump from one to the other. That is what I propose to do by decoding the grammatical elements first. The hops are smaller and by and large it takes less work although more steps to reach your destination safely."

As evidence that semantical interpretations are, indeed, a central component of the way people understand language, Marcus points to psychological studies done on the neurologically impaired, especially the dysphasic. Two distinct patterns seem to emerge among those who have difficulty communicating. In one case, the patient becomes confused about how to put sentences together although he still has no trouble understanding information presented to him about the world. In the other case, the patient speaks perfect grammatical gibberish; this is apparently because while he still retains his knowledge of how language and grammar works, he has lost the ability to comprehend and express general world information. Citing both of these cases, Marcus says the studies show that those of us who deal with language adequately possess a clear-cut connection between our sentence diagramming skills and our ability to process world knowledge.

Marcus is particularly adamant on this central feature of his theory. The computer will abide no halfways, he says. If a machine is designed with all the general world knowledge that is available but no intelligence about grammar, he is convinced it will fail miserably in the long run. "Like it or not people use grammar to talk and understand language," Marcus says. "And if you want to build a computer that will converse with people, you damn well better build into it all the components that will enable it to understand people. No partial truths will suffice here."

Though Marcus is under little pressure to draw his theory into the blueprints of an applied device, as a creative scientist he is looking forward to the day when his natural-language-understanding computer will be used by people. At this point, Marcus has been able to instill at least a pidgin grammar into the computers he is working with and he claims his research shows that because grammar and syntax are so formal and formulaic, once the computer understands a few basic rules, it begins to generate a whole series of higher-level ones almost automatically. In short, he says, it is much easier to teach a computer grammar than world knowledge.

The first application of his research will occur in just a few years, Marcus feels. The huge data banks of information about customers, suppliers, inventory, manufacturing and so forth kept by AT&T, which are now accessed by keypunch operators typing commands peculiar to the computer, will become far simpler to work with because the computers will understand natural languages. Marcus's computer will be attached to the front end of the data bank, the part that people communicate with. So instead of using keyboard commands that are unreasonable and inflexible, human workers will be able to retrieve information from the computer in their own languages. One might say:

"Show me all of my files that are more than three months old," and after sorting through the files that the computer offers him in response, he can add: "Purge files one through three, fifteen, eighteen and twenty-two. Save the rest."

Although obviously utilitarian, these easier-to-operate data banks are admittedly more of a by-product than a goal for Marcus. Marcus doesn't view improving access to data banks as a very glamorous justification for his life-long work. His dreams of how his research will be eventually used are far more grandiose and futuristic; they concretely delineate how artificial intelligence will ultimately affect everyday life.

"In about ten or fifteen years, certainly by 2010," Marcus says, "monster computers with monster memories will fit on my thumbnail and cost almost nothing. So how are they going to be used? We know that people don't interact with machines all that well. And therein lies the real payoff for my kind of work. It will allow people to communicate with and use the power of these monster computers.

"Example One: You're in your kitchen. You put a pot roast on the microwave first shelf and green beans on the microwave second shelf. Now there's this little extra hole the size of a quarter on the front of the microwave; that holds a five cent electric microphone connected up to the tiny monster computer in the microwave. So you say aloud: 'Microwave, there's a roast on the top shelf and green beans on the bottom shelf. I'd like the meat done medium rare and the entire meal ready at six.' And you leave to play tennis for the day.

"Example Two: You're walking out of your house and you turn to your light switch, which looks like an ordinary one except for the little hole on its top where the microphone is situated. You say: 'Lightswitch'—you've got to use these appliances' names, otherwise they won't know which you are talking to—'I'm leaving the house. Give me five minutes to get to the car then turn off the garage light. Turn on the den light at around nine tonight. Turn it off at around ten and turn on the bedroom light five minutes later. Have the garage light go on at about eleven tonight. I expect to be home by then.' And you leave. The lightswitch proceeds to communicate with all of the other switches in the house and follows your instructions to a tee.

"These may be slightly trivial examples. But translate these applications into health care uses or the way the handicapped can take advantage of this technology and you see the inherent value for society in my research."

Marcus may consider himself to be a basic researcher far from the oppressive rat race of the device designers, but he also exhibits a humanism and a pride in his work which demonstrates an allegiance to more practical uses for his theories. Interestingly, his work also perfectly dovetails with AT&T's probable future course. A prime topic of conversation in the high-tech community concerns Bell's intentions as a computer firm now that it has been freed to enter that marketplace. Marcus's research highlights a likely scenario for Bell. What Marcus is doing is combining artificial intelligence with speech synthesis or, put another way, he is combining today's most advanced computer techniques with the most far-reaching communications technologies. AT&T has been the world's leading force in communications for a century and now has the potential to be a major player in computer design and manufacturing. The two directions of Marcus's research are perfectly in line with the twin themes of AT&T's current corporate scope. Insiders contend that combining a one-two technological punch that merges the highest technology in computers with communications is a likely strategy for the phone giant to embrace.

But precisely because of the breakup of AT&T and the loss of its monopoly status, questions are being raised about the future of Bell Labs. Now faced with ever-increasing competition, can the parent firm afford to freely fund a luxury like Bell Labs at such high financial levels and leave it to its own devices? For these next few years the answer is yes. The commitment is made. But Bell Labs and AT&T officials refuse to consider how they would answer the question in five years. They prefer, they say, to avoid imagining the effects on corporate morale and identity of losing Bell Labs as they have always known it.

Still, all philosophical discussions and ruminations about the future aside, a visitor to Bell Labs at this point continues to feel well out of range of the manufacturing arm of the company. Little mention is made of the parent outfit by the researchers and there is almost no attempt to hew to any kind of corporate party line. Not so at IBM's research facility in Yorktown Heights, New York. There, one researcher's appraisal of his *raison d'être* at IBM was quite simply, "You're supposed to be doing research on stuff that is pertinent to manufacturing."

The IBM center is less daunting than AT&T's. Tucked into two hundred acres, right off of a major New York state highway, its campus is a nondescript, flat, almost pure-looking wooded tract, a correct match for the surrounding rural community of horse farms and vegetable gardens. The research building itself is not flashy; it is a low-lying, sprawling edifice that, because of the additional construction at the end of its wings, seems to be expanding its reach measurably. Inside is a workmanlike air. A concentrated, purposeful tone prevails among the researchers, not as collegiate as AT&T's.

IBM has been the prima donna of the computer industry since the computer became a marketable item, and the firm's deep involvement with artificial intelligence currently is a natural outgrowth of its wide-ranging research efforts over the years. In fact, IBM has consistently sought the cutting edge of technology, perfecting it and honing it into model artifacts before using it in real-world applications or offering it to consumers. Considering this, it is not at all surprising that one of the major artificial-intelligence efforts IBM is now involved in is one of the discipline's most difficult: automation research, or the development of intelligent robots with widely diverse skills. The Automation Research section at IBM has been in existence since the late 1960s. What started out as a small five-member group has now sprouted into an important component of IBM's research facilities with fifty scientists.

Mark Lavin is one of the senior members of Automation Research and is a leader of its work in machine vision perception. He arrived at IBM in 1979, a graduate of the Artificial Intelligence Lab at MIT. His studies at the university were influenced by Whitman Richards and the other theorists interested in the psychology of seeing. Though he has an academic background, Lavin feels comfortable with IBM's constraints on his work.

"The underlying limitation we work with here is that what you are doing has to be of scientific significance and have some practical applications at IBM," says Lavin. "So we in manufacturing research tend to be tied pretty closely to all the manufacturing divisions of IBM, listening to their needs and trying to work toward helping them overcome their problems. But I don't feel that we are influenced the wrong way. It is actually a healthy environment. Being in this environment we have a nice validation system for our work, because we get to try it out in real-life situations. This is lacking so many times in the academic world."

The first major robotics work at IBM was conducted under the auspices of an ill-fated project called Autopass, begun in 1974. The intent of Autopass was to build a robot that could accept a set of short-phrase commands from its human colleagues and then act on them with no additional prompting. This was to circumvent the need to formally program a robot's computer each time it has to shift tasks, a time-consuming process that is also quite labor intensive. The idea was to obviate the need for a group of computer programmers and robotic control supervisors on a job at all times.

"With Autopass, so it was planned, a user would be able to tell the computer: 'Take the cup and place it so that the handle of the cup is aligned with the right side of the table,' " says Lavin. "The system would have to be able to plan everything from how it will grasp the object to the path of travel and trajectory of its arms all the way down to what the individual motors should do."

Unfortunately, while it was universally recognized as a powerful idea, it was by and large scrapped by 1979 because it seemed impossible to bring to fruition in a short period of time. As one IBM researcher put it: "Just the problem of deciding where to grasp an object is difficult for a robot. Only now are we starting to feel even a little bit more comfortable with figuring out how to do that. How were we ever to solve all the higher-level technological questions Autopass was asking?"

Nevertheless, Autopass had a positive influence on IBM research. It generated some very interesting work in machine task planning and inspired a raft of research based on all of its separate components, much of it still a part of ongoing major efforts at IBM.

Mark Lavin is involved in two of the Autopass spin-off areas: developing three-dimensional vision perception and teaching robots to create their own plans of action from a simple set of instructions. He and a group of colleagues are attempting to combine these two aspects of intelligence and create a machine capable of taking sensitive, factory quality-control measurements.

"An awful lot of work goes into looking at parts in a factory environment to verify that they conform to the specifications and tolerance ranges as listed on blueprints," Lavin explains. "A lot of people are being paid a lot of money to do this. More significantly, even if you pay people a tremendous amount of money to do these jobs, they are probably not doing the job that you want—they are essentially gauging the direction and speed of the horse after it's way out of the barn. In practice, you would want to do a dimensional inspection and measurement so quickly that as soon as the wrong cut is made you would recognize it as such and say this process is going out of specifications. So there is a real press to try to automate dimensional measurements from the point of view of cost and speed."

Up to now there are nonintelligent machines capable of making low-level measurements, but it's still the task of the human being to do the intelligence work: to pore over the blueprint, gauge the intended tolerances of the parts and come up with the best quality-control scheme quickly and at appropriate times in the manufacturing process. It is the intelligence-dependent portion of this scenario that Lavin is trying to transfer onto the robot and its computer. "What we want to do is be able to say to the computer, 'Here's a model of the part including its tolerances; here are some low-level measurers that are available to you—perhaps a time-of-flight range finder, a triangulating range finder, a contact probe, etc.—now generate the best program you can to use these tools and go out and make that measurement.' The machine will do what I claim people do implicitly; that is, form a detailed inspection plan."

Considering the state of artificial-intelligence research today, Lavin's goal of having his machine in operation within the next few years is not at all unreachable. The robot will only need relatively simple three-dimensional vision because the machine will already have a strong model in memory of what the part it is searching for looks like. The factory environment will present few unexpected visual surprises and the parts will be in unoccluded settings with strong backgrounds.

Furthermore, the expert system that will complement the robot's vision will require only a few simple rules. The computer will have to know what each measuring device is used for and how to analyze what the device perceives about the part's dimensions and tolerance. It will also, of course, have to understand blueprints and specifications, another fairly simple task to teach to a computer. Essentially, Lavin is integrating some very primitive artificial-intelligence technology into an eminently practical device.

"Most of the IBM manufacturing plants can use what we are developing," Lavin says. "In fact, this is the kind of thing that an awful lot of industry is interested in right now." The message is pointed: The research will give IBM a leg up on its competitors in developing the factory of the future and allow it to retain its privileged position as a manufacturing giant.

While IBM and AT&T are perhaps making the loudest noises, at least financially, in their efforts to develop artificial intelligence, they are by no means alone in this field. Major corporations from all over the industrial marketplace are investing huge sums of money in the discipline. At the current stage, however, almost all artificial-intelligence research undertaken by companies besides IBM and AT&T is involved with expert systems, a technology that has already proven to be efficacious and would seem to represent a wise monetary investment at this point. Indeed, within this limited domain, the range of systems being developed is broad.

Some examples:

*General Electric has designed a locomotive troubleshooting expert system that emulates the expertise of a forty-year-veteran train mechanic. The expert system, being used at the firm's railroad manufacturing and repair yards, is already turning marginal and mediocre mechanics into competent ones.*

*Schlumberger, the oil-service giant, is developing an expert system that will be capable of interpreting complex data from oil-drilling devices.*

*Westinghouse is creating an expert system that will literally plan the sequence of manufacturing operations in factories. This computer will be able to choose from among thousands of schedules to enable its factory to process hundreds of manufacturing orders at once and efficiently.*

Technology has always been a powerful mover and shaker of industry. Correctly incorporating the most advanced technologies into corporate plans is the driving force behind the emergence of many growth companies, and the failure to do so accelerates the decay of many former leading corporate powerhouses. Artificial intelligence is just one new technology to be reckoned with. But by its very nature—specifically, its attempt to harness intelligence to a machine—it offers perhaps the ultimate industrial weapon. As the scuttle for position in this field at AT&T, IBM and the myriad other firms clearly shows, very few far-thinking companies are looking upon artificial intelligence lightly.

Chapter 8

# THE HUMAN VARIABLE

As quiet as it has been, the development of artificial intelligence represents arguably the most compelling technological revolution in our history. Since their first attempts at tool making, people have moved inexorably closer to the machine as an intimate and further away from their natural state. Creating smart computers can be seen as perhaps the final chapter in marrying people to their tools. It is a conscious attempt to finally close and lock the gap between us and machines.

Very few artificial-intelligence researchers seem to fear taking such a step because the payoff is felt to be so significant. Usually people's inventiveness has led to either increased ability to confront aggressors, improved economic conditions or expanded dissemination of knowledge and information. Artificial intelligence, by contrast, offers all three results. Some random examples:

*The millions pouring out of the defense establishment for artificial intelligence is a statement that the battles of the twenty-first century will probably bear little resemblance to twentieth century warfare. The real generals and strategic thinkers in a war one hundred years hence may, indeed, be computers—and not people—crashing wits against their counterparts on the enemy side.*

*The much-publicized factory of the future, sporting fully automated design and manufacturing, made possible by machines with artificial intelligence, is set to arrive. With its appearance, the industrial revolution will be shocked out of its long-lived first stage, which saw the machine as only an instrument of brawn, possessing no intelligence.*

*Agriculture, a decaying industry that relies on old tools and increasingly expensive labor, will be overhauled and turned over to robots for everything from fruit harvesting to sheep shearing. There is now, in fact, an annual Robotics and Intelligent Machines in Agriculture conference devoted solely to the theme of bringing artificial intelligence to the farm.*

*Information, from the most comprehensive reference works to pulp novels to yesterday's newspaper, will be available on home terminals, accessed by computers that understand language as people speak it. For example, you will be able to command the computer to search through all the books in the Library of Congress for every citation relating to either the Black Sox baseball scandal of 1919 or Black league ballplayer Josh Gibson; and then tell it to write a summary report and have it ready by five that evening.*

This list could be easily supplemented. Consider the discipline's potential impact on health care, in which diagnostic expert systems will complement the knowledge of physicians; on education, where computers will set up individual tutorial lesson plans based on each student's ability to learn; on social welfare for the isolated and the disabled, who will be able to use intelligent machines as companions and physical therapists; on politics, where computers will accurately assess the ebb and flow of public opinion and present reports to influence decision makers.

Artificial intelligence reaches across a wide spectrum. Indeed, no other single technological development has ever presaged such a great change in the quality and organization of life. At its deepest level, what artificial intelligence stands for is an entirely new relationship between man and machine. This time, the machine may actually become man's equal. And that opens up a veritable world of issues connected to how the intelligent machine will affect humans and their continued evolution as conscious beings.

In terms of intelligence, we have never had a match. People have always looked at machines as something either totally under their control—like the television set or telephone or even the personal computer—or as sinister, evil forces to be watched closely—like the huge computerized data bases that decide our credit ratings, send us bills or monitor our tax payments. The computer with artificial intelligence, though, fits neither of these categories. It is a machine of soft technology. Its mechanistic attributes are almost invisible, far from view. Being able to speak and understand natural languages will give the intelligent computer an organic, civilized texture in its interactions. Indications are that it takes very little prodding for people faced with intelligent machines to abandon the adversarial or master/slave relationship we have had with computers up to now, and take part in far more personal dialogues with them.

There is a well-known story in artificial-intelligence circles. It concerns ELIZA, a program that mimicked the responses of a Rogerian therapist. It was developed in the early 1960s by Joseph Weizenbaum, the MIT professor who later rejected it as an elaborate, but unintelligent, programming trick. Shortly after it was introduced, a well-respected computer scientist from the Soviet Union sat down in front of the terminal to have a turn with the electronic therapist. After some polite introductory banter between the machine and the man, the Soviet scientist began to divulge intimate details to the computer about his relationship with his wife, totally oblivious of the incredulous onlookers around him.

This exhibition of the power of artificial intelligence—even at it most primitive and inexact level—worried Weizenbaum considerably. "I had not realized," he says, "that extremely short exposures to a relatively simple computer program could induce powerful delusional thinking in quite normal people." If people are so willing to pull down the barriers that separate us from the machine, offering relatively little resistance, what are the ultimate implications of such an abrogation? Some see only dire consequences.

"There is the fear that increased technological sophistication may reduce the uniqueness and centrality of the human species in our general vision of the world," says Neil Frude, a psychologist from Wales and a long-time observer of artificial intelligence. "There is the suspicion that important social functions requiring human sensitivity and judgment will be transferred to the unfeeling machine. And there is an anxiety that artificial systems may come to usurp the position of human beings in our personal lives, leading us to prefer sham social contact with machines to real social interaction with people."

Ultimately, others add, the redefined relationship between man and machine may lead to severe over-reliance on the computer, because it is so capable. Stephen Andriole, the veteran artificial-intelligence computer designer who is building expert systems for the Army, says he has seen decision-planning programs created for the Pentagon that analyze in dollar figures the loss of an aircraft and a pilot's life when estimating the efficacy of a strategic maneuver.

"Now how the hell do you estimate the dollar value of a pilot, a human being?" he asks. "My fear is that the human element will get lost and the people working with the computer will simply take the machine's decision as gospel.

"All the individual has to do is sit back and watch the computer make his decisions for him. There is no challenge. I really worry about that. Are we going to create an undermining of decision-making capabilities in the same way that calculators have undermined our mathematical skills?"

Others—including most artificial-intelligence researchers—do not see the advent of intelligent machines as dangerous as long as people enter this new relationship with their eyes open. People must not forsake their role in the relationship; they should bring their humanism and culture to any dialogue with the machine's stolid intelligence.

Despite how people will relate to intelligent computers, though, one thing is certain: These machines will automate and take over many of the jobs now performed by humans. There are no good estimates as to how many jobs will be affected, but most experts consider the impact will be significant. Assaying such a transformation of employment patterns is felt to many to be a wise course to take now, before it reaches crisis proportions.

Automation has been the economic planner's bugaboo for many years, and the arrival of intelligent machines promises to heat up the debate over its effects. Still, despite the longevity of the argument, it has not yet been proven that automation will automatically result in higher unemployment. James Albus, a leading robotics developer currently at the National Bureau of Standards, takes the position that artificial intelligence in the workplace, if implemented carefully, can, in fact, lead to more jobs. "There is no historical evidence that rapid productivity growth leads to loss of jobs," Albus says. "In fact, quite the contrary. In general, industries that use the most efficient production techniques grow and prosper, and hire more workers."

This would seem to be borne out by the case of the U.S. banking industry. Here, increased productivity resulting from automation during the 1970s has led to a diversification of services—and a higher demand for them. Consequently, banking employment during that decade has grown by 50 percent.

"There is not a fixed amount of work," Albus adds. "More work can always be created. The problem is not in finding plenty of work for humans and robots. The problem is in finding mechanisms by which the wealth created by robot technology can be distributed as income to the people who need it. If this were done, markets would explode, demand would increase, and there would be plenty of work for all able-bodied humans, plus as many robots as we could build."

Of course, implicit in all of this is that the employment shifts brought on by the arrival of artificial intelligence in the workplace will also mean a change in the type of work people do—and, indeed, in the time they spend doing it. Many of the more dangerous tasks and drudge work will be taken up by the new machines. Potentially, the jobs that people do will envelop the more human aspects of life. Increasingly, people will be involved in the service professions, such as social work, education, health care, sports and entertainment. And we will probably have more time for leisure activities.

Some artificial-intelligence researchers are calling on government to recognize that the future in terms of their discipline is not so far away. Plans should be made to deal with the effects of this changing world. Somewhat melodramatically, Nils Nilsson, a veteran artificial-intelligence researcher at the Stanford Research Institute, calls this period a "last chance window" to use an emerging technology for the betterment of society as a whole and not allow ourselves, this time, to be used by the technology.

"Retraining is critically important now," says Nilsson. "We must begin training for such automation-resistant human service jobs as teaching, family counseling, daycare and health care. We must also educate people in arts, crafts, literature, writing and sports so that they will benefit from their increasing leisure time. We should also begin to work much more earnestly on the many transition projects required to move us into the computerized, postindustrial age."

The tangible issues, the human implications, of artificial intelligence deserve careful scrutiny. If they are not debated and approached with purposeful skepticism, these issues will be lost behind the din of the workaday, insistent pace of the artificial-intelligence researchers poised on an ultimate technological threshold: teaching machines to think. But while integrating new technologies into mainstream society in general is cause for calculated planning, artificial intelligence carries with it some enticing baggage that goes well beyond any hard and fast societal policymaking. For in artificial-intelligence research, there is much to be learned about ourselves—our consciousness, cognitive skills and relationship to knowledge—as we build ever more enlightening mirrors of human thought on the quiet circuitry of computers.

Marvin Minsky of MIT, one of the leading philosophical voices in artificial intelligence, put it best: "Just as the theory of evolution changed our view of life, so artificial intelligence will change our view of the mind."

# FURTHER READING

*AI Magazine*. American Association for Artificial Intelligence. Menlo Park, Ca.

American Association for Artificial Intelligence. *Proceedings of the National Conference on Artificial Intelligence*. Los Altos, Ca.: William Kaufmann, Inc., 1983.

Bernstein, Jeremy. *Science Observed*. New York: Basic Books, 1982.

Campbell, Jeremy. *Grammatical Man*. New York: Simon and Schuster, 1982.

Dreyfus, Hubert L. *What Computers Can't Do*. New York: Harper & Row, 1979.

Feigenbaum, Edward A. and McCorduck, Pamela. *The Fifth Generation*. Reading, Mass.: Addison-Wesley Publishing Co., 1983.

Frude, Neil. *The Intimate Machine*. New York: New American Library, 1983.

Hodges, Andrew. *Alan Turing: The Enigma*. New York: Simon and Schuster, 1983.

The Institute of Electrical and Electronics Engineers. *Automating Intelligent Behavior Applications and Frontiers*. Silver Springs, Md.: IEEE Computer Society Press, 1983.

McCorduck, Pamela. *Machines Who Think*. New York: W. H. Freeman and Co., 1979.

# INDEX


ABDUL/ILANA, 141–44
Abelson, Robert, 120
acoustics, machine vision assisted by, 172, 175–76, 177
agriculture, robots and, 220
Albus, James, 224–25
algorithms, heuristics vs., 71–72
American Telephone and Telegraph (AT&T), 15, 183–184, 201–2, 203–12, 218
analogies, 13, 168
  situation-to-situation, 90–91, 92–94, 95–96
Andriole, Stephen J., 97, 101–6, 186, 188–89, 223
Arab-Israeli conflict, script of, 141–44
Army War College, 101–3
artificial intelligence:
  brute-force method of, 18–19, 20, 23–24, 26, 46, 71, 114, 157, 158
  conferences on, 15–25, 38, 57–58, 61, 99, 114, 186
  human variable in, 219–26
  media interest in, 58
  state of, in 1983, 58
  traditional computing vs., 67–68
  Turing test for, 37–38
Artificial Intelligence Corp., 67
Artificial Intelligence Lab, MIT, 154, 167–68, 213
artificial intelligence research:
  brain research aided by, 11
  early claims in, 13–14
  expert systems and, *see* expert systems
  funding of, 12, 16, 65–67, 145, 157, 182–218
  heuristics in, *see* heuristics

in late 1940s, 13, 57
Logic Theory Machine era of, 17–25, 38
second wave in, 39–68
Turing's contributions to, 26–38, 39, 40
Ashby, W. R., 32–33, 39
automobiles:
futuristic, 9–10
identification of, by Richards's computer, 176–79
robot assembly of, 150–52
Autopass project, 214–15

backchaining, 77–80
hypothesize-and-test process vs., 85–86
banking industry, automation in, 224
Barnett, Octo, 73
basal ganglia, 49
basilar migraines, diagnosis of, 87–88
Bell Labs, 203–12
academic environment vs., 205–6
binary programming:
of brain, 31–32
of computers, 29
Bolles, Robert, 12–13, 156, 157, 159–66, 174–75
botany, 35
brain:
adequate solutions to complex problems found by, 47
Ashby's description of, 32–33
asynchronicity of, 43
computer vs., 19–20, 43–44, 45–46, 47
as electro-mechanical organ, 33
flexibility of, 44, 46
injury to, 41, 43
internal pathways in, 20, 40
known from unknown distinguished by, 19–20
Logic Theory Machine vs., 19–20
memory tags used by, 20
mosaic theory of, 30–31, 33–34, 40, 41, 42
neuroscientific view of, 39, 40–52, 53, 56
parallel processing in, 56, 85–86, 173
postulated growth of nerve cells in, 34
as programmable machine, 18, 19, 29–33, 56
redundancy in, 41, 53
speed of, 43, 44, 155
Turing's description of, 28, 29–30, 34–36, 39, 40, 46
vision and, 154, 155, 156
*see also* nerve cells
broad-band sounds, 175, 177
brute-force programming method, 18–19, 20, 23–24, 26, 46, 71, 114
machine vision and, 157–59
Buchanan, Bruce, 107
*Business Week*, 58

Cain, Ronald, 12–13, 157, 159–166, 174–75
Cambridge University, 27
Carbonell, Jaime, 13, 90–94, 95–96, 136

Carnegie Corporation, 99
Carnegie-Mellon University, 13, 66, 90–91
Carnegie-Tech University, 15, 17, 98–99
cerebral cortex, 41, 42, 49, 52
chemistry:
  Dendral and, 100, 106–9
  Fermi Project and, 95–96
  structure elucidation in, 106–108
chess-playing programs, 21, 23–24
Cognitive Systems, Inc., 67, 118
color recognition, 177–78
"Computable Numbers" (Turing), 28–29, 31
computer design, expert systems used in, 59, 72
computers:
  as artifacts of twentieth century, 69–70
  binary programming of, 29
  brain vs., 19–20, 43-44, 45–46, 47
  as knowledge engineers, 109–113
  in performance mode, 21–22, 38
  speed of, 43, 194–95
  synchronicity of, 43
  transferring analogy theory to, 92, 93–94, 95–96
  *see also* expert systems; robots
Congress, U.S., DARPA and, 187–89, 190, 192
congruency, programming concept of, 93–94, 95
Control Data, 66
counting out, 23
cybernetics, 13

Dartmouth University, 66, 67
  Summer Research Project on Artificial Intelligence at, 15–25, 38, 57, 61, 99, 114, 186
Defense Advanced Research Projects Agency (DARPA), 65–66, 182–200
  Congress and, 187–89, 190, 192
  as Defense Department agency, 184–85
  Information Processing Techniques Office of, 183
  Strategic Computing Program of, 190–97, 199
  unworthy projects funded by, 187–88
Defense Science Board, 65
demons, memory, 126–29, 134, 148
Dendral, 100, 106–9
  Meta-, 109–13
*Design for a Brain* (Ashby), 32–33
diagramming method, 61–62
dictionaries:
  in expert systems, 61–62
  in machine vision, 158
  scripts and, 133
diesel-engine repair, expert systems used in, 59, 72
disabled, computers used by, 221
Djerassi, Carl, 107

education, impact of computers on, 221

ELIZA, 22, 222
embryology, mathematical theory of, 35
emotions:
in mosaic brain, 30–31
in scripts, 143–44
*Encyclopedia Britannica*, 30
Enigma machine, 27
expert systems, 58–63
analogies used by, 90–91, 93–96
as artifacts of high-tech era, 69–70
for chemistry, 95–96, 100, 106–113
frame-based, 86–90
generic legal syntax in, 109–110
hypothesize-and-test process in, 85–87
knowledge engineers essential for, 96–97
knowledge in context of, 70–72
linguistic limitations of, 59–63, 116
for locomotive troubleshooting, 217
for making measurements, 216–17
military use of, 97, 195
one-domain limitation of, 90–91
for petroleum industry, 59–60, 61, 218
for physics, 95–96
as prototypical applied scientists, 70
rule-based, 75–84, 86, 117, 195
*see also* medical expert systems; scripts
Explorer, 61

factories:
of future, 220
robots in, 64–65, 150–52, 153, 164–65, 166, 215–17
failed predictability, learning by, 123–25, 126
Feigenbaum, Edward, 12, 67–68, 70, 71–72, 74, 97, 98–101, 106–13, 117, 199
Fermi Project, 95–96
Ferranti Mark I, 35
Fifth Generation computer project, 67
frame-based expert systems, 86–90
Frude, Neil, 223
FRUMP, 140

General Electric, 217
General Motors (GM):
and artificial research funding, 201
press conference of (1984), 9–10, 14
generic legal syntax, 109–10
genetics, 35
geology, expert systems and, 59–60, 61, 218
geometry, expert systems' knowledge of, 93–94, 95
Giamatti, A. Bartlett, 118
goal satisfaction, 20
heuristic reasoning used in, 48–50

grammar, 115
  diagramming method and, 61–62
Greenaes, Robert, 73
gulls, vision in, 171

Haase, Kenneth, 167–68
hardness, computer assessment of, 178
heuristics, 12, 48–50, 69–113
  algorithms vs., 71–72
  analogies and, 90–91, 92–94, 95–96
  backchaining in, 77–79, 85–86
  in chemical, analysis, 107–13
  defined, 48
  and hypothesize-and-test process, 85–86
  in Kent's pipelined-image-processing device, 54–57
  as key to cognitive modeling, 71–72
  knowledge engineer's role in, 96–113
  in medical diagnosis, 72, 74–83, 87–90
  memory indexing as, 94–95
  in meteorology, 83–84
  in military, 101–5
  as operand of human intelligence, 71
  visual, 50–57, 172, 179
Hewlett-Packard, 200
hippocampus, 41
Hoevy, Edward, 119–20, 130, 135, 197–98
Honeywell, 66
House of Representatives, U.S., Armed Services Committee of, 188–89
humor, scripts and, 125–26
Hunter, Larry, 145–48
hypothesize-and-test process, 85–86

infections, heuristics used in diagnosis of, 75–82
Integrated Partial Processing (IPP), 130–41
  Hunter's program vs., 147–48
  Logic Theory Machine vs., 138
  precursor of, 140
intelligence, human:
  heuristics as operand of, 71
  intelligence needed for imitation of, 37
  uniqueness of, to individual, 36
  Young's quantification of, 33–34
International Business Machines (IBM), 15, 183, 192, 200, 201, 202–3, 212–17, 218
  Automation Research section at, 213–17
introspection, 23

Japan:
  Fifth Generation computer project in, 67
  Ministry of International Trade and Industry (MITI) of, 197
Johns Hopkins Hospital, 52
*Journal of the American Chemical Society*, 112
Jungian psychology, 34

Kahn, Bob, 182–83, 184–85, 189, 190–91, 194–95
Karsberg, Tina, 142–43
Kawasaki Heavy Industries, 150–152
Kent, Ernest, 13, 46–48, 50–57
key words, in ELIZA program, 22
knowledge engineering, 96–113
  as bottleneck in creating expert systems, 97–98, 106
  computers doing work of, 109–113
  methods used in, 100–101
  quality of expert systems and, 96–98

language:
  binary, 29, 31–32, 116
  as key to mind, 115
  *see also* natural-language research
language scripts, *see* scripts
lasers, in robotic vision, 157, 161
Lasker Award, 42
Lavin, Mark, 213–17
leaf embryology research, 35
learning by failed predictability, 123
Lebowitz, Michael, 130–31
Lederberg, Joshua, 107
limbs, mechanical, 152–53
Local Feature Focus, 159–66
Logic Theory Machine, 17–25, 99
  brute-force method as basis of, 18–19, 20
  human mind vs., 19–20
  inflexibility of, 23–24
  IPP vs., 138
  Kent's pipelined-image-processing device vs., 54
  knowledge in context of, 70–71
  Turing test and, 38
Lynch, Gary, 41, 44, 45, 94

McCulloch, Warren, 13, 31–32, 39
Manchester University, Computing Laboratory of, 35
Marcus, Mitch, 204–12
Martin Marietta, 200–201
Maryland, University of, 87
Massachusetts Institute of Technology, 21, 66, 67
  Artificial Intelligence Lab at, 154, 167–68, 213
mass spectrometry, 107–8
mathematical theorem solving, 17, 20–21, 24
medical expert systems, 10, 59, 79–90, 145–49
  for diagnosis and treatment of infections, 72, 74–83
  for diagnosis of basilar migraines, 87–88
  frame-based, 86–90
  for oncology, 145–49
  pulmonary, 82, 145–49
memory, computer:
  accessing analogies from, 13
  brute-force method and, 18–19
  frame-based expert systems and, 89
  machine vision and, 158, 161

memory, computer (*cont.*)
videodisks and, 146, 147, 148
virtual, 183
memory, human:
language scripts and, 121, 122, 123–24
physiology of, 41
recalling data from, 20, 94
and redundancy in brain, 41, 53
vision and, 170
memory (programming) demon, 126–29, 134
memory indexing (tagging), 20, 94–95, 155
language scripts and, 121
Meta-Dendril, 109–13
meteorology:
heuristics used in, 83–84
scripts and, 123–24
Microelectronics and Computer Technology Corporation (MCC), 66
military:
expert systems and, 97, 101–105, 195
robots in, 65, 191, 194–96
translation programs and, 186–187
*see also* Defense Advanced Research Projects Agency
Minsky, Marvin, 24, 25, 226
mosaic brain, 30–31, 33–34, 42
Motorola, 66
Mountcastle, Vernon B., 41–42, 51–52
Music Cognition Program, MIT, 167
Mycin, 72–83, 85–86, 96, 149
as advisor system, 145
backchaining used by, 77–79
slowness of, 82

National Science Foundation (NSF), 199
natural-language research, 60–63
ABDUL/ILANA and, 141–44
at Bell Labs, 206–12
diagramming method and, 61–62
IPP and, 130–41, 147–48
memory (programming) demons and, 126–29, 134, 148
neomodern linguistic theory and, 62–63
scripts in, 120–49
at Yale, 116–45, 147, 149
Nau, Dana, 87–88
nerve cells:
"all-or-none" character of, 31–32
arrangement of, in cerebral cortex, 52
chemical packets released from, 44–45
mechanistic model of, 31–33, 35–36
in mosaic brain theory, 30–31, 33–34
mutative and plaint relationship among, 44
postulated growth of, in brain, 34
nerve impulses:
speed of, 43, 44
threshold levels and, 44–45
Newell, Allen, 13, 17, 54, 70, 99
*Newsweek*, 58

Newton, Isaac, 51
*New York Times*, 58
Nilsson, Nils, 225–26
nuclear magnetic resonance, 73

Office of Cybernetic Technology, DARPA, 186
oncology, script-based artificial intelligence and, 145–49

Pacific Medical Center, 82
packet switching, 183–84
parallel processing, 56, 85–86, 173, 195
performance mode, computers in, 21–22, 38
Pershing missile, 197
physics, Fermi Project and, 95–96
pipelined-image-processing device, 52–57
Pitts, Walter, 13, 31–32, 39
pixels, 158, 160
plant genetics, Turing's work on, 35
Poggio, Tomaso, 168
*Principia Mathematica* (Whitehead and Russell), 17
programming (memory) demon, 126–29, 134
psychotherapy, computer-simulated, 22, 222
public opinion, computer analysis of, 221
Puff, 82
pulmonary-function testing, by expert system, 82

radar, computerized, 193
Rand Corporation, 15, 17
range-finding, structured-light technology, 161–62
RCA, 66
redundancy:
  in brain, 41, 53
  in Kent's pipelined-image-processing device, 53
reference libraries, 220–21
Reggia, James A., 83–90, 96, 179
relevance, programming of, 23
restaurant scripts, 120–23, 124–125, 126–27
Richards, Whitman, 154–55, 168–181, 213
Robotics and Intelligent Machines in Agriculture conference, 220
robots, 10–11, 64–65
  agriculture and, 220
  Autopass project and, 214–15
  in factory environment, 64–65, 150–52, 153, 164–65, 166, 215–17
  human senses integrated in, 64
  military uses of, 65, 191, 194–196
  vision in, 64, 152, 153–54, 156–181, 194, 196, 215, 216–17
Rose, Steven, 45
Russell, Bertrand, 17, 51

Schank, Roger, 12, 24–25, 62–63, 114–20, 144–45, 148–49, 179, 186, 187, 199–200, 205, 207
Schlumberger, 201, 218
*Scientific American*, 30

scripts, 120–49
of children vs. IPP, 139–40
emotions in, 143–44
humor and, 125–26
inferences and, 128–29
IPP and, 130–41, 147–48
and learning by failed predictability, 123–25, 126
in machine vision, 172
in Marcus's computer, 207
and medical diagnosis, 145–49
memory (programming) demons and, 126–29, 134, 148
and quantifying value of new information, 125, 126
as static memory-and-information packets, 123–25
as vehicles for information, 122
semantics box, 206–7
semiconductors, very-high-speed, 194–95
Senate, U.S., Armed Services Committee of, 188–89
Shortliffe, Edward, 72, 73–75, 117
Silicon Valley corporations, 70
Simon, Herbert, 13, 17–19, 20, 54, 70, 98–99
situation-to-situation analogies, 90–91, 92–94, 95–96
Slade, Stephen, 130
social welfare, impact of computers on, 221
Soviet Union, space program of, 183
spectral video machines, 178
speech synthesis, 211
Sputnik, 183
SRI, 156–57, 164, 192; *see also* Stanford Research Institute
Stanford Medical School, 73–74
Stanford Research Institute, 12–13, 156–57
Stanford University, 66, 67, 70, 72, 100, 106, 107, 157
Star Wars concept, 192
stock brokers, electronic, 21
Strategic Computing Program, 190–97, 199
structure elucidation, 106–108
supports, machine vision identification of, 175, 176–177, 178–79
Symbolics, Inc., 67
symbols, Jungian, 34
synapses, 45

Teknowledge, Inc., 67
telecommunications, 184
telephone-line troubleshooting, expert systems used in, 72
teleradiology, 73
temperature sensing, machine vision assisted by, 172
templates:
knowledge engineers' use of, 104, 111
in robotic vision, 158, 160, 165, 170–71
terrorism, IPP's script on, 130–141
Texas Instruments, 192, 200
translation (movement), machine vision identification of, 176, 178–179
translation programs, 63, 119, 186–87

Turing, Alan M., 13, 26–38, 51
brain as viewed by, 28, 29–30, 34–36, 39, 40, 46
as early computer designer, 27, 28–29
as embryologist, 35
as military decoder, 27
test for artificial intelligence developed by, 37–38
Young's correspondence with, 33–35
Twenty Questions, visual, 172–174, 179–80

Ullman, Shimon, 168
ultrasound technology, 73
unemployment, automation and, 224
Urata, Kenji, 150–52

venereal diseases, Mycin and diagnosis of, 81–82
very-high-speed semiconductors, 194–95
video cameras:
in Kent's pipelined-image-processing device, 52, 54
robotic vision and, 157–58
videodisks, as computer's visual memory and output, 146, 147, 148
videotape, knowledge engineers' use of, 101, 104
Vietnam War, 188
virtual computer memory, 183
vision, computer, 12–13, 152–167, 168–81
acoustic sensing used with, 172, 175–76, 177
brute-force method and, 157–159
color recognition with, 177–78
current state of, 153–54
heuristics in, 50–57, 172, 179
identifying supports with, 175, 176–77, 178–79
Local Feature Focus and, 159–166
in pipelined-image-processing device, 52–56
range-finding, structured-light technology and, 161–162
Richards's contributions to, 154–55, 168–81
in robots, 64, 152, 153–54, 156–181, 194, 196, 215, 216–17
three-dimensional, 215, 216
visual data bases for, 160, 162–164, 165, 170–71
vision, human:
inferences from, 173–74
Local Feature Focus vs., 160, 165–66
memory and, 170
parallel processing in, 173
stereo, 168
universe organized with, 154–156
visual cortex, 49

Wang, Pearl Y., 87–88
warfare:
future of, 220
heuristics in, 101–5
use of expert systems in, 97, 101–4, 195
Weizenbaum, Joseph, 21–22, 38, 222

Westinghouse, 218
Whitehead, Alfred North, 17
World War II, 27

XYZ coordinates, 161–62

Yale University, 66, 67, 114
  natural-language research at, 116–45, 147, 149
Yessner, Raymond, 145–46, 147–148
Young, J. Z., 33–34

# ABOUT THE AUTHOR

JEFFREY ROTHFEDER is an investigative reporter who specializes in high-technology and environmental issues. He has written for *The Washington Post*, *The New York Times* and the *Bergen Record*, and was an editor at *Electronic Design* and *Personal Computing* magazines. Currently, he is the editor of *Medicine & Computer* magazine.